THE FIELD OF TRANSFORMATIONS

A QUEST FOR THE IMMORTAL ESSENCE OF HUMAN AWARENESS

THE FIELD OF TRANSFORMATION

BIKA REED

A QUEST FOR THE IMMORTAL ESSENCE OF HUMAN AWARENESS

Inner Traditions International, Ltd.
Rochester, Vermont

Inner Traditions International, Ltd.
One Park Street
Rochester, Vermont 05767

Library of Congress Cataloging-in-Publication Data

Reed, Bika, 1931–
  The field of transformations.

  1. Egypt—Religion. 2. Spiritual life. I. Title.
BL2443.R43 1987 299′.31 86-20163
ISBN 0-89281-154-4 (pbk.)

10 9 8 7 6 5 4 3 2 1

Distributed to the book trade in the United States by Harper and Row
Distributed to the book trade in Canada by Book Center, Inc., Montreal, Quebec

Typography by Royal Type
Designed and produced by Studio 31

Printed and bound in the United States of America

TABLE OF CONTENTS

I dedicate this book to Methethy, the "chief of the Royal Farmers of King Unas." I stood in the dark hall of the Brooklyn Museum, unaware of time, so much was I struck by the gaze of his obsidian pupils. And as the keeper pushed me gently toward the door, a question rose in my mind: What kind of a field did such a man plow?

Acknowledgments

I wish to express my gratitude to Robin Lipsy, for his invaluable help in the process of the preparation of the book for publication; to Christopher Bamford, for his dedicated and skillful editing; and to Ehud Sperling, for seven years of waiting.

Preface

While trying to comb Maud, an old, black, shaggy dog whose fur was unreasonably matted, I realized that my task of writing this book could only partly succeed. Much of the unredeemable fur had to be cut off, like the rational connectives which the reader might expect.

The essence of the present work concerns the relationship between rationality itself and its inconceivable "I" of intelligence. This relationship is paradoxical and even absurd. But then, paradox and the absurd have always appealed to me, and this attraction led me, finally, to the door of ancient Egypt. I grasped the relevance of ancient Egypt's understanding of life and creation to the philosophical impasse in which our world seems to be. For only there, in her sacred writings, could I find the serene, mystical heart of an intelligence which functions as a unity through a system of duality.

This book is not a study of ancient Egyptian myths, symbolism, or history. It is an attempt to present Egyptian thought to the modern reader by distilling it from its mythical core. Such an attempt demands a redefinition of the concept of intelligence and the reanimation of its living crystal of synthetic intellect, which unites the many contradictory facets of psyche and intelligence, inaccessible to reason alone.

The synthesis of rational and emotional intelligence is the scriptural seal on the sacred Egyptian writing, which keeps its contents undisturbed by time. It is only through the regeneration of these contents in the reader, however, that this book will gain meaning and existence.

I am Shu, the creator coming forth from his own self. I come forth through my utterance as the ruler of the flesh created from its own self.
[*Revelation of the Soul of Shu* 2]

PART I

The Foundations of Awareness

It is I, at the heart of cycles, who am the lord of the lord of the green fields in the beyond. [*Rev.* 15]

CHAPTER 1

Self-Conception

Thus I sink into the Shrine and surge
from it as he who creates himself.
[*Rev.* 29]

The Carnival

There is a particular atmosphere of febrility and excitement
at the end of a year, or cycle, be it a civilization, a season, or
a single human life. For such critical moments, ageless
rituals and customs once existed to channel the excitement
through feasts, where both pain and joy were exalted. The
passage from death to rebirth was ritually mimed—brutally
and gaily, without sentimentality. The old king, the ruler of
the time that was ending, was represented by an effigy
which was mercilessly destroyed. A part of it, however,
was preserved until the next year's carnival. This part was
the link, the hidden *measure* and safeguard against total
destruction. In many old legends we find that the dragon is
never utterly destroyed. The ritual act of *measure* unites all
acts of measure as a token of the mystical oneness of the
destroyed, the destroyer, and the newborn. It is a physical
remnant, representing the past whole, and thus it is a relic
and a ferment. It also represents an act of restraint in
destruction, a measure taken by an irrational force in the
collective psyche of man. This force is the pacemaker that
protects its shrine in man through a ritual fusion with what
seems absurd and yet enables him to go beyond the rational
limitations of his singularity. Thus, like a hidden drummer
stimulating man's vitality at a time of natural fall, the spirit
of a time-cycle celebrates, by means of carnival rhythms
and high jumps, the communion of flesh and mind.

Until recently, in the French province of Quercy, also
called the White Land, the carnival started with the ageless
cry: "*A carnival si mangia di car.*"* The words *white* and *red*

---

* At Carnival, one eats flesh.

took on the meaning of death and resurrection, tinted with blood. In a mock coronation a white bull was crowned with laurel and taken for a triumphal walk, at the end of which he was chased, slaughtered, and sacrificially eaten.

There is something extremely moving about an unaware victim placidly awaiting his slaughter. Western man, as the engendering force of the new world, is now facing his moment of bloodshed like the white bull. Crowned with the laurel of progress, and lured like a mock leader into a procession, he listens to the mournful cries of youth, echoing amid amplified rhythms. His industrialized entertainments and sciences, like an injection, prepare the necessary passive state of mind for the end of the parade. This anticipation of spiritual slaughter is supported by the whole social and economic net. In his incapacity to grasp the depth in himself, man today is like a blind dancer endlessly trying to hear the beat which is lost in the confused sounds of nature. Following his own heartbeat, he steps nearer and nearer to the abyss.

There is nothing so eloquent as the edge of a precipice. How else could man realize the height to which he has risen? His intellectual evolution is a peak from which he sees nothing but the ravine. This king of knowledge, in his hopeless striving for lost youth, spreads despair over younger generations. Upon his throne, the intellectual is weak from want of any true understanding of life. Joyless in his power over a confused world, man, like the weary time-god Saturn, ordains his own carnival.

While in archaic societies Saturnalia were a form of ritual sacrament and led to purification, today they are performed unconsciously. The carnival atmosphere is present in the taste for excitement, pseudo-idealistic and pseudo-religious sects, sexual overindulgence, and anarchic mass murder. Burning the old effigy, the carnival spirit springs up like a formidable dwarf from the ashes. In its high jumps it engenders the clownlike fashions and hairstyles, a love for the absurd and for gratuitous originality, the worship of mangy heroes, and the derision of formality. But where the ancient festivities commemorated order by ritually introducing measure into a feast which stimulated frenzy, today this ageless, spotted laughter is becoming a dangerous smile, preying upon order itself.

In the Saturnalia, convicts became kings for only three days. Today, freedom is claimed by terrorists as part of constitutional human rights. Bloodthirsty pagan customs involved the sacrifice of one chosen animal as a token of communion in blood. Today, we sacrifice entire species, forests, rivers, and seas to the idols of our sophisticated materialism. According to ancient ritual, the villain-king was dethroned after his brief rule so that social order could be reestablished. Today, it seems that the carnival is out of hand. Our villain-king is a phantom. Hailed by the somersaulting of clowns, he smiles softly, an atom bomb in one hand and a book of prayers in the other. Like a falling curtain, our time is bringing the stage games to an end. The firecrackers are bombs; the blood is real. Unaware of the lever in the trap door, man points triumphantly at his discovery of a dark opening in the rock of life. He prepares to reap the harvest of long research by laying hands on hidden treasure. Yet, penetrating into this cave like a one-eyed pirate, he stumbles on the ground of the great fire-blower. Only by stepping closer will man realize that he is the straw man. And, while the primordial stone closes down upon him, he will respond to the call that made him penetrate into this hidden shrine and impress his experience of life into the eternal seed of divine transformations. This remnant of his life survives the fiery baptism as the ferment that will give life to the new priesthood emerging in man.

> I am the dweller within the million
> beings. [*Rev.* 7]

The Two Destinies

Today, intellect is on the threshold of a new dimension. Standing on the frontier between nature and her unknown destination, like the baboon on the frontier between animal and man, intellect confronts the hostile wilderness of a congenital solitude. Both baboon and man have lost the innate knowledge which manifests the harmony of life on earth. Instead, they have gained a fierce curiosity and a tremendous capacity for adaptation. But while this capacity protects the baboon as a species, enabling it to adapt to practically any food or environment, this same adaptive capacity exposes man to unknown danger by urging him to forsake his ecological security as a species and to go against his tribal wisdom as an individual.

Through the natural birth of intellect, the self-protective function at the core of nature creates a self-destructive threshold of transformations which leads intelligence away from nature.

Intellect is a form of intelligence unknown to nature: the intelligence of meaning. The evolution of this intelligence may be seen both as the disintegration of nature and as her creative transformation. Through this transformation, meaning fixes its own imprint on nature. Man, as the bearer of intellect, naturally feels that it is his birthright to be above nature. But in spite of this, as the fruit of nature, man suffers death. The drive for individual affirmation creates a desire in him to be more than a biological procreator. Nevertheless, he pours his procreative fire endlessly and blindly back into nature.

Enclosed within a field of conflicting forces, his field of transformations, man is constantly dying, constantly being reborn. Like a spider, which in order to attach its web in midair builds its suspension bridge over the abyss between two precarious leaves, man builds his castle between the two poles of his inner division: his doubt and his inner knowledge. His intuition causes him to feel that his life is eternal; his reason negates this. Thus man challenges himself to face the painful reality of the simultaneity of opposite truths in his own being.

While aware reason cannot identify itself with anything in existence, intuition identifies man with all natural realms. We often say that man is an animal. But although man is moved by animal drives and survives physically like an animal, we could equally well say that man is a mineral or a plant. For man, like the earth, is a multidimensional structure of ageless sediments. The past of unknown, preceding worlds is inscribed in him. His mind, like an old rock, contains petrified forests, lava, crystals, and fossils that trace the long-forgotten agonies of extinct species. Man's structure is apparently solid, yet it is a field of constant transformations. Processes that take millions of years to occur in nature are embodied in his daily metabolism, by which he not only transforms his food into biological sustenance but also transforms his organic energies into the *functional qualities* of his awareness. Like a plant, he gradually transforms mineral and organic life into a new mental being, which is foreign to nature. By such synthesis, man not only incorporates natural transformations in his metabolism but also summarizes the gradual evolution of an abstract intelligence of creation from primordial collective preawareness to individual awareness.

In man, organic functions as a synthesis of all preceding stages of evolution become aware intelligence. In this way, through man, nature receives her fruit, which, like all fruit, carries its seed.

Man has two destinies: one as perishable fruit, another as the imperishable seed of an abstract intelligence that leads nature to her end. The word *end* has a double meaning which joins the concept of goal or striving with the concept of discontinuity. This expresses man's twofold destiny. By evolving, he disrupts nature, yet his intelligence represents nature's evolutionary goal or end. The evolutive seed, coming to self-expression in man, liberates itself from its perishable base in the form of conceptual intelligence. *Although he receives his body from nature, man, identified with aware, conceptual intelligence, can be seen as prior to nature.* In comparison to nature, man's physical life is short, yet his intelligence, as the abstract seed of all nature, is eternal.

> His arm (of self-destruction) is my own scepter, living in my enemies in the sky or in the earth. I expel them from their hidden place. I overthrow them in their fortress. I destroy them from within their own base. I break their authority from within their establishment. I transfix their vital force. I dismember their mind. I reduce them to slavery. [*Rev.* 36]

Infinity and Reason

Infinity, as understood today, is a rationalization placed in time by reason of an intellective experience which is not rooted in reason. Through such rationalization of the natural experience of man's divinity, divinity itself is reduced to its definition. Placed in time, both concepts, infinity and divinity, lose their status of experience and become imaginary ideas. Reason, in this way, cuts the umbilical cord between man and his origin. The idea of a "God in the sky," resulting from this separation, is parallel to the idea of infinity as an endless expansion of matter within time and space. Placed in time, infinity becomes part of time. "Space-time" is thus promoted to the status of the self-creator, logically generating atheism as a form of new "religion."

This new religion, although not admitting that it is a form of religion, creates the worship of the inertial principle at the origin of expansion.

Historically, monotheism marks the enthronement of singularity, through the evolution of reason. The "I am," abstracted from its all-encompassing quality and reduced to the logical subject of the principle of objectivity, has gradually drawn a circle round itself. Reducing the fugitive spiral of its inconceivable self to a plain definition, "I am" moves the history of intellect in two directions. On the one hand, it exalts the rule of egocentrism. On the other hand, as the preaware conceiver of its self-conception, reason creates the elements of a new intellection, closer to geometry than to natural talk. Through reductionism, abstract concepts are created. These concepts, in spite of the fallacy which has generated them as definitions of the undefinable one, nevertheless offer themselves to a different interpretation of their meaning.

The relationship between existence and meaning manifests itself at the root of human mind as an "I" which is aware of reason. Reasoning alters with time. This is observable in every human being and in civilizations. These alterations are not identifiable with the evolution, within reason, of meaning or self-conception. The spontaneous cosmic and natural cycles form a concentric, specific pattern of individual manifestation of their synthesis in every individual awareness, like a mental fingerprint. Through this fingerprint alone, all cosmic relationships are drawn into a vortex which is man and can communicate as a system of balance, within the "I" which thus conceives itself.

Every revelation of the inconceivable oneness of the multiplicity which constitutes existence is a fingerprint within eternity, the self-conception of meaning. The role of reason, as the carrier of the relationship between existence and meaning, is crucial. But this crucial position is not a natural

cross. The difference between the crucial position of awareness within the universal balance of life and the cross
through which this balance becomes a word of meaning, is
the subtle essence of all initiations.

The crucial position of awareness within existence is a
potential cross with several meanings. Although implying
some form of crucifix, it also is the foundation of the edifice
through which the knowledge of the crucial position of
reason within life reaches its own reason. Thus reason
alters with time but evolves through the cross.

> I gain awareness from the million beings.
> [*Rev.* 7]

The "I"

Sitting in his room, man can think and create a whole world
according to his premeditation. In his mind, he can build
magnificent cathedrals without crowding the outer, galactic space. His premeditation is an abstract "space" which
alters its contents without altering man's features or the
wholeness of his organic life. As an aware thinker, he is
enclosed within a substantial being belonging to a substantial universe. But, at the same time, his awareness is an
"I" and one with the inconceivable "I" whose premeditation substantiates the world in which the aware thinker is
born. Within this secondary "I," as the crucial point within
existence, the self-conception of the primary "I" is the
potential cross: the re-reversal of the principle of self-
conception, which is "space-time," into meaning. This re-
reversal enables reason to conceive the galactic space as a
space of premeditation within the divine, inconceivable
"I." The natural a priori of space and time is not destroyed
in the act of the reversal. It is included, like memory itself,
in a new meaning.

The difficulties arising in the process of the evolution of human understanding of life are rooted in the very essence of understanding which is the aware thinker. Although he can feel, and thus intuitively understand existence, he cannot conceptualize his intuition, except through reason. In its role of conceiver, reason is nature's spontaneous definer and, as such, it manifests the radical force of the natural seed. Through this force of measure nature shapes and channels its creation. In man, seated within awareness itself, the measurer becomes reason. On the scales of reason, weight and measure are the base of the equational quantification through which reason functions as both reductionist and conceiver.

Is divinity situated in life, or is life situated in divinity? Am I within the system of balance which is my body, or is this system of balance in me? But how can I be within me, when this "me" is I? The absurdity of that situation of the egg within the chicken and the chicken within the egg is the essence of the cross through which the natural a priori of reason challenges its own reality.

The word *within* denotes a relationship of size, and when we use it in an abstract sense it still pulls our natural reason into the logical reactions it would have had if it dealt with a relationship of two sizes. This logical tendency of assessing the container and the contained by physical standards adds another note of absurdity to the question. By natural standards, something can only be "within" something else if they are two things, not one. The second thing should automatically be smaller than the first; otherwise how could it fit? The very fact that we are posing this question—Which of two given things fits into another?—already predisposes our reason to react by challenging our sanity: it should be self-evident. It thus seems naturally self-evident to us that the invisible, be it infinity, divinity, or "I," should fit within the body which is visible, and, for this reason, should be considered bigger.

In the same way that space acts in its reason as the definer of size, time reflects the law of ruling all phenomena and our own existence in the inborn chronology through which we grasp the beginning and the end. Chronology is the essential sustainer of the natural thinking process, through which we sort out what comes first and thus are able to produce definitions.

This unanswerable riddle, often formulated through the question "which came first, the chicken or the egg?", truly concerns us all. It points to the simultaneity of two inter-related phenomena, each evidently posterior to the other, which gives some spice to the absurd task of trying to find out which is the first.

The riddle of the hen and the egg illustrates both phenomena. It is also humorous to reduce the absurdity of the situation of reason within its physical existence of an amusing joke. The essence of the riddle is, however, less amusing, because it is the cross between natural speech and abstract thought. In natural speech, which reflects natural life, the "egg" is only a physical egg, and the hen, in the same way, is only a physical hen, while in abstract speech, the "egg," as a concept, may be the symbol of existence. The "hen," as it happens, did not as yet, have the privilege of being adopted by philosophers as a symbol of the philosophical egg. The riddle places this real hen in connection with the egg of creation, and this mistaken relationship causes the riddle to become unsolvable. Because if we did have the particular hen in question in front of us, we would answer that she is older than her egg. Or, if we saw the egg of that particular hen we would say the egg is older, having in mind the natural time after which the egg becomes a chicken.

When inciting people to fight, the leaders of war usually promise to solve similar riddles. But when they win their war, they say: "There are no easy solutions." Reason, as the leader of humanity, does the same. In many popular riddles and jokes, a sinister form of promise is mixed with a prediction of the cross. In its radical imperative, reason is man himself, the aware "I" of an ageless, crumbling rock which carries its own wholeness of chronological and structural sediments in its consciousness as a feeling of pressure and weight. Man's own inconceivable self is at his mercy, like a beggar at his feet. This divine beggar in man cries tears which are the burning flood of the baptism of self-conception.

Ancient civilizations spoke of the invisible sun as the origin of awareness, not at the source but at the mouth of creation. They spoke about the abyss, the ancestor of man, as a primal manifestation of the invisible sun. They spoke about physical existence and the physical sun as the body and heart of the self-creator. The saints and heroes who died in the formation of our new world left testimonies of their visions which were not so far from the scriptural testimony of the ancient world. The hierarchy of angels guarded and surrounded God, like the mystical principles surrounded the bark of Ra. They were the reflections of the system of balance through which divinity manifests itself. Conceiving divinity through a system of balance turns reason away from impersonating divine power. But reductionism, in its growth, burned its scientists in public places and spilled blood to enthrone a single almighty god who reflects reason. In response, the surviving scientists became even more radical and lit a potent fire under the feet of the church. Engendered in the bosom of the alchemists, rational intellect is today the awakening dweller within its own premeditation: the fiery baptism through which individual reason must pass—a lone traveler.

Older than his vegetating fields . . .—I am
at the root of mysteries. [*Rev.* 20]

CHAPTER 2

Premeditation

I bring to the dweller in his vault his own
crown. I draw my kingship from his substantiation. [*Rev.* 23]

Preaware Premeditation

When we naturally accept the fact that a whole tree, animal,
or man evolves from a seed according to its specific form,
we unwittingly accept more than we realize: a principle of
transformations, of which man's evolution is the perfect
expression. We accept an irrational fact: an apparently *mate-
rial substance* as the solid state of a *genetic intelligence*, a whole
life, with all its chronologies codified and invisibly folded
into a solid substance.

Every seed is a living proof of the existence of creative
thought. It thereby reveals that animation or life arises from
an unrecognizable and abstract form of *premeditation*.

Intelligence, which intellect reveals when it understands
the laws of nature, is inscribed in nature, bound to creation,
and exists prior to intellect itself. This intelligence is one
with creation, which manifests it as its own procreation
(intellect), and one with its abstract seed (premeditation).
Every form of metabolism leads, however unrecognizably,
to the emancipation of a specific, functional quality from its
physical matrix in the process of the exaltation of nature's
intelligence. This emancipation, in its turn, serves as a base
for further transformations which conclude in their synthesis in man. Thus, beyond its observable states as a structural, seedlike reality, *premeditation*, in its abstract essence,
may be identified with the principle of creation, procreation, or evolution itself.

We may find it difficult to think of a seed as premeditation. We are accustomed to consider it only as a function of
human awareness. We define premeditation as thought,
which precedes and plans an act. Although it may be a bad
adviser, premeditation is the chief function of man's aware-

ness, bringing him supremacy over nature. Yet one cannot deny that all organic nature and its behavior evolve according to conditions set by the seed. Observing the precision of this evolution, we may conclude that the essence of the seed is preaware and abstract premeditation.

We attribute animal behavior to instinct. But a seed's behavior cannot be qualified as instinctive, only as *preaware*. For premeditation, although reflected in our aware intellect, does not originate there. If it did, we could never have been born by means of a seed (sperm) and ovum, which, in a "premeditated" way, evolved into a fetus, a crying baby, and a thinking human being. The evolution of intelligence in man rises as a network of interrelated, organic functions evoking the classical image of the cosmogenic egg of creation containing its premeditated dweller.

The evolution of this dweller in man's awareness cannot be understood apart from its egg or creation. The egg, in its turn, has no philosophical meaning without its premeditated essence, the dweller. Both egg and dweller are inseparable from the principle of the seed, of which they are both proportional individuations or ratios.

Man's two destinies reflect the two interdependent streams of creation: inertia and animate intelligence. One is the bow; the other is the arrow. Inertia with its mindless reactivity is the bow, the eternal curve of cycles. Evolving intelligence arises out of it as the seeker, the ever-rising arrow. From the curved bow of the earth, the tree of life is born as an arrow. As the arrow, life projects itself into death. Yet from this curved movement toward death, which acts as the consumer of all the fruit of life, the seed springs again, projecting itself beyond death like an arrow of living intelligence.

In man, the bow of inertia and the arrow of intelligence edify the face of their hidden archer. For although the abstract intelligence of cyclic existence acts universally as the inanimate creator of life's perishable fruit, it also creates within this perishable fruit the *condition* for the self-projection of its imperishable essence from it. This *condition* is awareness arising in man as the first (primary) manifestation of the archer—the *spirit* separated from its state of premeditation.

> O gods, your mind does not evolve through your own utterance, but through me alone. My becoming is the force of the entire creation, which flows forth from the Word of the great Lord "This." [*Rev.* 28]

The Hidden Steps

Life on earth emerges as a fragmentary trace of abstract, continuous movement of the evolution of intelligence from mineral to mind.

Observing the strata of animation traced by the different realms—from the mineral through the vegetable and animal to man—we can define these by their function in the overall structural process of creation resulting in man.

The mineral world is like a sleeping hand, reckoning and slowly sorting out its own future body. It is a dreaming god, rising through the slow whirlpool of its awakening to take hold of the world which it creates. The main aspect of this elementary creation is *sorting out*. Elementary qualities are extracted from chaos and joined together into groups of active elements on the basis of repulsions and affinities.

In this primordial movement, the twofold function of absorption and assimilation emerges, creating qualities by separation, and then joining them together into groups to form the invisible basis for the structure of the world. Although all selective movements of repulsion and affinity may be seen as the forces of chemistry or physics, these are essentially *choice*, manifesting the principle of intelligence. This is *life-giving thought* as active premeditation in its primordial, mineral aspect.

Unlikely as it seems, the mineral realm, unrestrained by form, is one with the flow of the primordial thought. It is the perpetual, invisible movement: the founder of life. Crystal and rock grow indefinitely and crumble away again. Clouds of gases constantly change consistency and shape. Like a huge wave, the mineral earth turns upon herself, gathering her seminal force.

Stepping into the vegetable realm, we can follow this seminal force rising vertically from its horizontal base (the structural plan of the exaltation of organic intelligence). Plants and animals are modeled into definite shapes which represent limitations of the creative flow of intelligence. A vital archetype thus emerges from its "foundation stone" in the mineral realm. The twofold function of absorption and assimilation, manifesting the primary selective, mineral intelligence, now emerges as the root-function of nature. From a root rises a stem, branches, and finally a head. This head is first a blossom, then a fruit, then a seed.

The opening of the blossom is the natural symbol for all opening of potential. The fruit is the natural symbol for all transformation. In the enclosure of the fruit, the plant's opened potential matures and withers. It becomes detachable and rots to yield the seed. The seed is the final contraction of the initial opening of the plant's potential and the final outcome of the destruction of its fruit: the natural symbol of synthesis.

Although it is the final contraction and the conclusion of a cycle, the seed is at the same time the potential reopening of a new cycle leading to a new seed. Beyond its solid form, the seminal force of the seed can be seen, like the mineral, to be an invisible inner movement. Yet unlike the mineral foundation, which in its endless accumulating and crumbling moves inertially, this movement of the seed is a shaper of life, proceeding by contraction and dilation like an earthworm. Every contraction is the destruction of fruit. Every dilation is the life of a new plant. This abstract movement through the formation and destruction of complex metabolic structures is the secondary, vegetative aspect of the *life-giving thought: the preaware search for definition.*

This abstract movement of the seed could be visualized as a radiant stream, constantly circulating through the plant, guiding its transformations toward an inscription or definition which is the synthesis of its existence and the cause of a new life. The moving chronology of the plant's life is contained in the stillness of the seed.

Without disrupting its indefinite mineral base, the vegetative intelligence rises in search of structural definition. Thus without disrupting its vegetative foundation, animal intelligence rises from the vegetative definition of its creative principle.

Emerging from the vegetable realm, the evolution of animal species traces the steps by which the preaware intelligence of creation moves toward structural *individuality*. Like a great river which breaks up into streams and splits into a million droplets of a cataract, life always sustains the moving wholeness of its water which is *preaware thought*.

Preaware thought, inherent in all life, produces the living balance through which substances grow, constantly altering their form and chemical constitution. The cosmos maintains its balance through the dilative and contractive phases of stars and galaxies. The earth maintains its own balance through the life of nature and the cyclical path of the seasons. Organic creation maintains its balance through the structural edification of man, by which it expands its contractive, defining principle of intelligence.

Qualities of potentially intellective articulation emerge gradually as a net of organic functions from their forked root of absorption and assimilation. Life expands, creating and manifesting a balance of interacting systems and cycles. These evolve through nature into a single organic structure, which embodies the balance of this interaction in an aware thinking organism.

Maintaining its generative balance and relying on the perpetuation of its creative *ferments*, life-giving thought monitors the evolution of its aware *thinker*. These creative ferments are the *qualities* of the universal seed of life, which is life-giving thought. Reflected in the primary mental functions and generated through the physiology of species, they are interconnected as nature's "mind" through the round of predators. Through the natural chain of predation, different breeding and feeding habits unite all realms, creating an abstract system of balance: the "ruler of the chemistry" of preaware intelligence. This is nature's concealed mind or "head," premeditating its future revelation in the human mind or head.

Whereas the creation of species appears as an observable chain of natural development, the unfolding of the principle of individual awareness, the *thinker*, moves unobservably through and beyond it like a hidden stream within the ocean. Undisturbed, his stream traverses matter and nonmatter, life and death.

In death, as in all destruction of fruit, lie the assimilative stages of hidden transformations. These stages mark the potential qualities of the principle of individual awareness as it matures through the contractive and dilative phases of evolution. Dilating phases may be seen as the creation of the species, contractive phases as their death or extinction. Thus the awakening of the thinker within creation moves, as a causal chain, from effect to effect.

Each contraction is a reorientation of the force of expansion—a restriction which causes a new phase of growth. As a fetus grows in interacting phases of constant development, so the evolution of the revelation of the premeditated thinker proceeds through the interacting realms of one genesis.

Cosmic elements are interconnected into realms and, within realms, into species. Within each realm, "species" generate the *key qualities* of preaware thought. It conceives and transforms them, however, according to its own *premeditation*, thus creating the hidden steps of its evolving thinker. One may visualize this potential thinker as moving through interrelated species in leaps, as a child runs down a stream on stepping stones.

> Through his Word he creates his existence, yet he does not complete his evolution, for it is I who re-create the wholeness of his body and his soul.
> [*Rev.* 28]

The Ancestor and Individual Affirmation

Within the eternal rise and fall of nature, in its repetitive chronology, a hidden movement rises out of its gyratory permanence in the mineral, vegetable, and animal realms. This movement has an evolving hierarchy, which manifests itself through the drive for individual affirmation and comes to awareness in man.

Looking about us, we can observe species of animals and plants which have subsisted for millions of years without changing. We can also observe the simultaneity of different species and, within individual species, the variety created through adaptation. We can observe, furthermore, a variety of human cultures and the simultaneous coexistence of both primitive and sophisticated societies. We can find traces of geological changes, extinct landscapes and animals. We can find skeletons of extinct species that lived in landscapes not noticeably different from those we see today. This discrepancy in *age* between parts of life coexisting on earth shows that evolution is neither a uniform nor a one-sided process. We may conclude, from observation of the present and all the known past, that chronology will never give an answer to the enigma of life, since chronology exists only in time, and time is the effect, not the cause, of creation.

Evolution orients the reproductive systems of plants and animals toward individual reproduction. While simple plants live and function as collective beings, complex plants generate *individually structured seeds*. Families of plants and species of animals represent a hierarchical structure. From simple monosystems, complex structures evolve, forming more and more perfect expressions of their realms. Thus we find the synthesis of the vegetable realm in the fruit-bearing plant, and that of the animal realm in the mammal. Within and through realms, we can observe evolution as a thread which moves not as a chronology but as a hierarchy of structural development.

The interrelationship between realms demonstrates that the evolution of life is based on the development of a metastructure. It also suggests that the emergence of life itself on earth could only manifest as a primitive system of balance and therefore a harmonic simultaneity of the elementary mineral, vegetable, and animal realm. Differing trends of evolution represent the creation of the parts which will find the condition of their synthesis in the human mind.

As a prism breaks up sunlight, the broken-up complex of life reflects the activation of its inconceivable seed. From this natural foundation, particular species evolve as interdependent developments of the functional parts of man. We can see primitive and evolved animal structures in human cells, plasma, organs, and muscles and in the nervous system and cerebral complex. We can trace individual species as parts of man. Indeed, evolution itself is traceable as the interconnection of functions embodied in the human organs. Every human organ has a long history of its own within the evolution of species. Thus history cannot be separated from the *function* that this organ has assumed as part of the human metabolism in relation to man's brain. This potential relationship between metabolism and its articulation could also be said to be the condition for the revelation of their abstract, original oneness, that is, their *ancestor*.

Man, as the functional synthesis of all realms, articulates the abstract seed of their common origin. Only through man's cerebral complex can realms enter in communion and so form a perfect sentient being. As parts of an invisible, living jigsaw puzzle, they are included in a meaning originally unknown to them. Through evolution, the preaware intelligence of creation forges a physical seed that embodies a plan for the manifestation of its abstract origin. Thus nature's evolutionary process can be understood only through the human metabolism, and species can be defined only through the place they occupy in the formation of the endocrine glands, nervous system, skeleton, and organs of the human being.

Aware thought functions within a system of polarity and crossing. Through the mirror maze of man's brain, new orientations of natural functions arise that are isolated from nature. Left and right, up and down, constantly rotate like a living cross in man's head. Although in many ways he looks like the rest of the earth's creatures, *man's mental life is based upon a principle of reversal, through which nature's functions are drawn into meaning that is foreign to nature.* Growing spirally around the pituitary gland and ramified through the skeleton, organs, nervous tissues, and blood, the human organism is a moving network of threads drawn from nature into the stream of a single intelligence. Through crossing and recrossing, every fiber of man's organism represents a crossing point new to nature and a thread which must obey the law of its hidden loom. One with the stone and with the darkness and depth which he draws to himself like a root, man surges from this loom as the negator of nature. For he is the link between nature and the revelation of the meaning of her inanimate transformations.

The revelation of this meaning is the hidden animator of man's intellective evolution—an animator manifested in creation through the drive toward individual affirmation which engenders the force of adaptation. Thus evolution does not arise from adaptation. On the contrary, the capacity for adaptation originates in the principle of individual intelligence evolving through nature. As a natural occurrence in plants and animals, *adaptation is the prefiguration of aware intellect in preaware organic life and the animal psyche. Man's aware psyche is the platform upon which potential individuality, lying behind adaptation, manifests itself through its quality of deliberate choice.*

Whereas the harmony of nature survives through a genetic restraint of individuality, man's survival depends on individual behavior. Only in man does adaptation as a natural protective quality act through intellect, altering his understanding of life. Thus in him individuality assumes the role of the mutator of the natural chemistry of preaware intelligence.

> I became the weaver in the flesh of the ancestor who creates himself from himself. [*Rev.* 11]

The Condition of Choice and Mutation

Within the framework of evolution, the capacity to change behavior according to circumstance and environment, that is adaptation, can only be consistently recognized as a manifestation of individual intelligence. It would be logical to assume that it increases with an evolving organic structure. Yet this is not always the case. For example, the more a plant evolves, the more its survival depends upon the individual seed, and thus the more restricted it becomes by conditions and the less adaptable it is. A similar restriction is observable in the more evolved animal species, whose young cannot survive without care and protection. It appears that in the course of evolution, with increasing degrees of autonomy, new relationships are created between the individual and its seed. Individuality, conditioned by its dependence on learning, is both strengthened and endangered in relation to nature. Continually moving through nature, this interrelationship between seed and individual emerges in man as a platform from which he can fall or edify himself. *This self-edification through realms and species, of an organic condition of aware choice may be seen as the hidden origin of human individuality. It is also the origin of the capacity of adaptation in nature, which allows a surge of individual behavior within species.*

The harmony of natural life is sustained by the unalterable seed of the species, which ensures the perpetuation of constant interspecies relationships. Within the framework of a defined species, both procreation and adaptation can be seen as the guardians of the natural balance. It is difficult to imagine that adaptation, as a self-protective function in animals, could be the cause of the creation of new species— as it is held to be neo-Darwinian theory—for if it were, it could neither act as a protective agent of established species nor act at random to create the genetic reorganizations observable in the steps of evolution.

Tracing the occurrence of the adaptive capacity in nature, one can easily be led to interpret it as the force underlying the mutation of species. In fact it represents, on the contrary, a natural obstacle. In the same way as the joints of the body, surrounded by liquid, are pliable and allow relative freedom of movement, so a degree of learning within genetic limits and a degree of adaptation cushions the links between interrelated species. This occurs without causing the structural changes which would dismember the body of nature if they happened at random.

The archaeological search for the missing links between evolutionary stages can be compared to the search for the Holy Grail with a metal detector. For only in the human being can these links be traced as functional crossing points within the structural division of his brain. Through this division, the two interrelated streams of nature's intelligence—inertia and animate intelligence—face each other as two animate selves of a new causal phenomenon of nature: an aware "I," rising as their uniter.

Within the structural complex of man's psyche, primary mental functions, as key qualities of nature's evolution are channeled and related, through a maze of disconnections and reconnections, to the aware "I." This aware "I," which appears as the outcome of these functions and the consequence of this maze, reflects like a mirror its own preaware conceiver: an *inconceivable "I."* For human understanding (the conceptual intellect) evolves through stages like life on earth and reveals, beyond its maze of both man himself and nature, its divine identity.

> Unborn, I am older than birth itself.
> [*Rev.* 14]

The Spirit of Premeditation

Man's intellective evolution rises like a wave from its ocean of breath. Within this living ocean in which each part is unaware of the other, the gaze of man's natural awareness is foreign to its own root, which generated it, and foreign to the universe which contains it. Surrounded by differing inner realms and cycles, this gaze is sustained by their harmonic interaction. Its flesh is made up of myriad cells that live and die unknown to it. Its bone carries its flesh and speaks to it in the mute language of the blood by which the circling structures of lymph, hormones, and nerves communicate with further circuits of subtle energy. Each of these circuits functions both as a whole and as a part of a larger whole: a realm of nature in man with its own period of decay and regeneration.

In nature the preaware thought is a *sleeping ancestor* who rules creation through the hermetic autonomy of each realm and the unalterable laws ruling the interrelationship between realms. Although interconnected, cosmic and natural realms do not communicate through aware choice but only through sleep and death. Death is the bed of the sleeping ancestor. In his sleep, like a giant swaying from one leg to the other, the ancestor gives rise to the potent reverberating murmur of nature, the echo of his immutable dance. Under his feet, nature's great order is eternally rebuilt. All living creatures obey this murmur, each following their own unalterable movement like colonies of ants and bees. As animals always repeat the same innate gestures that are rooted in this murmur, so men endlessly repeat their secret vows, hopes, and angers. Although springing from the same source as animals and plants and subjected to the same repetitive laws of sleep and death, *man reflects these laws differently from nature, whose clarity derives from the lack of direct communication between her realms. By his awareness, man veils nature's clarity.* His gaze, traversing nature's depths, meets the abyss at the crest. Moving against nature's preaware roots within his flesh, man communicates unknowingly with his true origin—the abstract radiant *eye* of premeditation.

The distance between this radiant *eye* and man's mental *eye* of aware intelligence is immeasurable. This is why it is the abyss. Yet this abyss, which man bears within him, is a primordial bond between him and divinity. Thus it is also a ratio and a sealed memory of man's inconceivable self. For this bond which joins man to his hidden origin is also the mystery of his spiritual seed. It both perpetuates the fixed, proportional patterns of all cyclic existence and escapes from them; it is both inertial movement and animate intelligence. This movement is the bridge between the *sleeping ancestor* and his estate. Animate intelligence is both the architect of this bridge and the one who traverses it. The relationship between the architect and the one who traverses the bridge is the relationship between the meaning and its own capturer. It is the seed-pattern which hampers the liberation of its original "I" and thus of man's transcendence. The capturer of its own self, transcendence, which builds itself a prison of seed in order to emerge from it, escapes definition in man. It is the carrier both of the inconceivable "I" and of its estrangement, which is the transitory, mental, aware "I." Through their relationship it manifests the Spirit of Premeditation. Thus the life-giving thought, solidified into seed, is manifested through the word which rises from it. The rising word calls forth the thinker, who emerges as the new measure within the effects of the balance which is the seed. The new measure overrides the original balance and becomes the measurer awakened from its self-induced sleep. Within man the effect of the seed, this measurer, acts as the self-creative regenerator of the memory of the inconceivable "I"—within its own oblivion, creation itself.

In the Self-Creator, it is I who am the
breath of all creatures. [*Rev.* 20]

The Hearing

By inhaling air, man enters into contact with a form of
intelligence which transmits itself as a feeling of breath.
Looking into the airy void which appears deeper in darkness than in sunlight, we could conceive it as pure, life-
giving thought, the mover of the immeasurable spiral of
life.

Within creation, the resonance of the preaware, life-
giving thought creates its *hearing*. This hearing, at the
origin of all forms of tropism and instinctive intelligences,
unopposedly rules the universal behavior of phenomena.
In man, however, it creates a cross between obedience and
understanding. Through his central nervous system, a
balance is set between the two poles of perception: the
preaware intuition and the aware reason. The mental a
priori of space and time that rules aware reason is the
ultimate expression of the unchosen limitation to which all
natural phenomena are subjected. In its codified field of
vision, as in a prison, reason by the virtue of its awareness is
doomed to become the rebel against nature. For nature is
both the only observable origin of reason and its mental
limitation, as well as the cause of its physical death. The
cross between reason and nature places man's intellect in
the process of transformation, through which it opens to a
new, *spiritual a priori*.

The all-pervading language of life-giving thought, vibrat-
ing and transmitting itself in waves of spatial impulses,
creates the polarity of action and reaction that rules matter
and energy, nature and man. Causing different reactions in
every part of its universe, this language is apparently a
"void," and yet it beams into its own creation and makes
itself understood by nebulae, stars, tigers, and trees. In

man it permeates all levels of his cosmic and natural life, revealing itself as the voice of his soul, rising from inspiration as an exhaled breath which is the Word.

> I am he who extends the heights of heaven. I am he who brings forth his own radiance by offering the force of his self-perpetuation to his divine ancestry. [*Rev.* 25]

Trismegistus

Upon entering life man draws his breath from an unknown source. Beyond his personal life, this unknown source acts within him as an "I" of the Spirit of Premeditation by which he lives. It never dies, although evolving into self-cognition it eternally experiences death.

This eternally recurring experience, brought by flesh to its hidden dweller as an inscription, lives within man's instinctive fear of death. His divine memory foresees the cry of this instant in which time dissolves within its own effigy, which is man. Through time, which is his genetic space, the hidden dweller links his fire of death to his night of transformations. Man's search for fearful excitement and excess in physical pleasure negatively reflects this ultimate embrace in which the hidden dweller, dying and reborn, merges as an eye into his radiant "I." For the human being is the bearer of both the divine memory and awareness, through which this memory forges its animated eye.

Human awareness is a living entity, which is not the organic man but an evolving "eye" of premeditation. Rising from its physical being, this eye in man's psyche acts as an entity and yet is a ghost, animated only by virtue of its organic structure. This organic structure links aware intelligence with the generative space-time that conditions the psyche as the concept of the reality of its own existence. Yearning to fuse with this concept, and thus substantiate it, the psyche fosters the divine substantiation in man. Thus the psyche may be seen as the field of subtle plantation. This plantation is the "papyrus" on which the Spirit of Premeditation inscribes its animate testimony.

Man is the substantial bridge between two insubstantial shores: preaware thought and its "I" of premeditation. Upon this bridge death is born as a concept. Only by assessing his mortality as the way to his immortality can man reassess his concept of "death." Instead of facing the end of his life as an execution, imposed by an unknown judge for no obvious crime, he now conceives his death as a sacrificial door to another dimension of intelligence. "Death" as a mental concept loses its original meaning when separated from physical man, its conceiver. In contact with the preaware conceiver of his own force of conception, this physical man conceives himself as the spirit rising from its premeditation. This conceiving of oneself as a new entity within oneself is the birth of a third vision (or "eye") within the secondary, natural intelligence of the aware "I," which is unaware of its origin. This conception represents a process of the gradual building and elimination of the mental "blocks" by which the Spirit of Premeditation gradually reveals itself to its natural progeny, man's psychic "I." This complex process of conceptual birth evolves in irregular frequencies of contraction and expansion.

The awe that man feels toward all that is undefinable and emotionally unrecognizable is the preaware response of a hidden "I" in his flesh. Stirring in its own depth of creation, as in a womb, it points like a compass needle to its abstract north of conceptual birth. The inner knowing of a wider dimension of being, in which man's awareness only partly participates, lives in all existence as a preaware code and memory. It surges in all creatures like a flash of lightning, warning them of danger and commanding flight or attack.

This natural warning system, common to all animals, acts in man according to his individual interpretation.

Man thus fears his indiviual *interpretation* of an instinctive danger signal and not, as is often said, the unknown. For he can only fear what he perceives on some level of his existence through natural affinities. What is not inscribed in him, and thus cannot be felt through affinity, can only leave him indifferent.

Man's individual interpretation of the meaning of life is reflected in the quality of his search for joy. In the rebellious stages of his mental evolution, he seeks excessive physical pleasure, creating a cult of sterility as an unnatural, mental death. In the phase of the reassessment of the foundation of his mental life, he meets solitude and silence as an unrecognizable call within him of the memory of a gestation prior to his own life. Through this memory he meets a new life promised by his search for joy. Thus a divine seed is shaped within man's mental self as the engendering cry joining death to life.

Indirectly, through his search for joy, man reconstitutes the steps of divine self-creation inconceivable to his natural awareness. His natural awareness reflects nature in him, and only through its intellective evolution can it become the retrospective witness of divinity. This witness rises from the cleft between the two sides of his intelligence, intuition and reason, conceiving itself within man's inspiration as the bearer of meaning. In physical existence, the birth of meaning is a second, conceptual birth, which may be seen as the womb for the ultimate, third self-engendering cry of the Trismegistus, born into imperishable life.

I shall call out: Silence, Lords of Time, issued forth from the ancestor of genesis. I reveal to you, O generations of myself, that I rule over my creation in the abyss. For I have seen the abyss becoming I. He knew not the place in which I became, nor did he see me becoming his own face. [*Rev.* 10]

CHAPTER 3

Revelation

> I do not obey spells. I precede them. It is I
> who give breath to life which surges from
> the Word of Tum, for he comes after me.
> I am the *ever-evolving* Self-Creator, the
> sole one who is older than the gods.
> [*Rev.* 24]

The Imperishable Self

As the planetary orbits trace and thus perpetuate an invisible testimony of the structural essence of their movement within their system, so human lives represent a testimony of spirit, rising from its structural premeditation.

Within intellect—the furthest point of genesis from elementary matter—the eternal noncreated sap of preaware intelligence reaches awareness, flowing interruptedly through the long stalk of its evolution as within the bloom. The aware individual "I" is the potential reader of the testimony of the self-generation of the inconceivable "I" from its cosmic roots through nature and intellect. The memory of this self-generation is inscribed as a genetic testimony in man's flesh. Beyond space, time, energy, or movement, the aware "I" is the only true witness of its own all-encompassing, inconceivable self.

Concealed within the shrine of its flesh, the inconceivable "I" is the dweller who depends for his manifestation on awareness—the mystical heart of man—which alone can open its shrine within the flesh. But this *heart* itself depends on the evolution of the synthesis between intuition and reason within intellect: the reckoner in the flesh, who builds his verdict gradually, as a river builds its delta.

Human mental life, from earliest youth, flows like a river, building its resistance to the dissolution which awaits it in the sea. This resistance creates a marshy delta in the mind of man, through which the "I" can channel dissolution into the cognition of its greater life, the sea.

Thus we can see in a river both the image of the natural flow of primordial energy in its unknowing search for dissolution and the image of the impetuous, unknowable imperative of the evolution of intelligence in its search for the *arcanum* of its own existence. Within this river of his double destiny as a perishable fruit and an unperishable seed, man, following his natural affinities, freely chooses the way to use his intelligence. Yet at the same time he unknowingly pronounces a verdict upon the way in which the unknowable imperative of his mystical self will manifest—a verdict which will rebound on him through the quality of his life and his death. Awareness, in its irrational movement, is drawn to a perilous adventure of its own kind. Like a sleeper upon a floating raft, it is carried with the outgoing tide into the depth of the turning sea, where man's last breath opens as a slow vortex to carry him back, as an unaware infant, into its unknowable self.

> I establish the Lord "This," to exalt the self-creator and reveal the sky as his inherent power and unity of all creative laws. Thus, inconceivable to the gods of creation, he edifies his name. [*Rev.* 12]

The Lord "This"

Man hungers for immortality, yet on his mortal terms: not as a birth into timeless existence as meaning, but as a prolongation of physical life. Timeless duration is the weightless center of balance, while prolongation is only extra weight on one side. Thus reason, dominating man's mental balance by the weight of rational argument, negates the supremacy of weightlessness, seeing it as an insubstantial counterargument. It weighs man down in the hopelessness of the misunderstood human condition. Reason sees this condition as the end of a line of nature which nothing follows. But we should rather say that nothing *similar* follows. For timeless duration, which is foreign to and yet contains observable existence, could never be conceived naturally by reason, which reflects existence only as its natural progeny.

The spheres of temporal existence within timeless duration abide in harmony, like a living chain of beings touching each other's fingertips. Through this long chain, timeless duration is present as blood is present in organic realms, animating yet not disturbing their sovereignty. Human intelligence coexists as a mental sphere with other spheres of intelligence, aware and preaware. Its hidden individual "I" contains it, being itself inseparable from the body, which is in its turn one with nature and cosmos, which is one with the timeless and universal "I."

Thus, when a child is conceived in the womb, it travels within its mother, who travels in the world, which travels in the sky, which travels within the cosmos, which travels within its womb of moving space, each moving in opposition to its container. And within that child, the "I," as the potential of a new divine name, revolves in the multidirectional genesis of its own space within the one duration of its all-encompassingness and responds to the exterior world and time. Like a drop of mercury in the swaying palm of a man hanging upside down in a boat rocking in the ocean, moved in its deep wave by the sky and in its shallow wave by the wind, so the "I" emerges from its own abyss between its time and its timelessness.

Sunk in preawareness as the seed of its reawakening, this "I" raises and lowers itself in all creatures in response to its measure which is the weight of existence. Thus, when a bird of prey drops, the "I" rises with its cry, and when the mountain goat lands on the other side of a crevice, the "I" rises in its grazing. In man alone the "I" emerges from the depths of his bone, an earthborn fledgling, seeking the sky, its heritage, in bounds and somersaults.

Through its time-born names, the "I" draws the inexhaustible potential of its being into its embrace. As the human embrace creates humanity, so the divine embrace generates the divine memory: the life-giving thought that is carried by its generative cry as a new "I," sinking in its own self-creation. And as man grows according to the memory of his seed, so galaxies, with all their worlds and systems, grow from memory of the abstract cry of a divine embrace. Beyond size, every form of creation is the substantiation of the resonance of the divine cry, opening and becoming a spiral space within the spaceless, timeless ocean of its divine original breath. Condensing within itself into turning clouds of gases and vapors and becoming fire and night which twist around each other like two blind snakes in their continuous and constrictive embrace, the divine cry generates the substances of its universal life. Through death, these substances seek their reintegration into the generative embrace of fire and night, their origin. All substantiated systems, from galaxies to individual organisms, owe their existence and ultimately their extinction to the constraint of an inner balance between fire and night. Extinction marks the exhaustion of every individual resonance of the primordial cry within its self-created void.

The intensity of this embrace, within which the perishable vanishes within the imperishable, is like the dream torn away from its dreamer: a living yet insubstantial and thus imperishable reality. In this inconceivable reality are rooted both man's fear of death and his ecstasy of life. Intellect, identified with the perishable in itself, perishes with it. Seeking this imperishable reality, it sinks into its faceless depth. There, suddenly, it reaches the new "earth" of its true belonging and hoists itself out of the sea which is time. This new earth is "This," through which awareness is channeled to reveal itself to its own eye as the seed of its further life. Intellect recognizes "This," which has always sustained it, between the two waves of its breath and in its *duration*, like the embrace which contains the opening and the closing of its two arms. This life-giving embrace is the merging of an instant of time into the timeless existence of bliss, promised to man through his experience of ecstasy in life. Through bliss, as through a doorway, man's awareness steps into its own focus. Visibility becomes recognition; light becomes clarity. Man recognizes meaning within its timebound world, as he recognizes thought within the "I," and understands light as the seed of clarity in the dark womb which is inspiring him. For clarity, immured in the foundations of man's awareness, yearns to penetrate the gravity of his earthly hunger, acting like a counterweight which moves the balance of his life. It is the force of the imperishable eye, rising from his breath.

Within this innermost embrace of defining fire of his reason and infinite night of his intuition, life and death meet in man as on a chessboard. Each man builds his own checkered space within himself as a springboard from which to escape time. Square by square, through interacting phases, man builds his own self-assessment. For in him the two opponents must become one victor. Within the turning abyss of his twofold mind, pressure surges like a fiery geyser from within the nocturnal soul. In him fire is an "I" which contracts, coagulates, and hardens into concepts. Night is the intuitive "I" which absorbs, dilates, and hides the true conceiver in its depths. In their synthesis this inconceivable conceiver reaches man's awareness as the invisible, inaudible pulse from a star reaches a snail or a blade of grass in the nocturnal prairie.

> I am "This" which breathes creation.
> [*Rev.* 11]

Inspiration

Whereas fire is the primordial cry of the "I," creating the depths of its space, air is the potential Word rising within the galaxy of fire. The Word is older than the cry from which it springs. As breath in search of its source, the Word reaches the mouth to become a voice rising from its pre-spatial, precreational, nonconceptual, and inconceivable inspiration. Inspiration thus generates its awareness as the "I am" which is existence, expanding by inspiring, and thus drawing into itself, as into the night of a crushing mouth, the potential exhalation which is the Word. Unceasing inspiration rules the vortex of all becoming from which surges the "I breathe" as a testimony of the inspired within the inspirer. Dying, man does not expire but inspires. He draws the air in, holds his last unreturned breath within him, merges into it, and becomes the breath.

From birth, man unknowingly seeks the meaning of breath. Throughout his life he breathes like a traveler stepping with each breath farther into the *instant* of timelessness, which, like a cleft between the two sides of his breath, remains the unrevealed animation of its "I," soothing and healing every cell of his being in a fusion of absolute belonging. By exhaling, man manifests through his aware thoughts the seed of this instant, which, like a timeless stitch of the divine presence, holds him together in time. Thus, ever new, he reaches the measure of his breath.

Through breath, the Spirit of Premeditation permeating the air reaches both man's brain and its own specified radiant salt of meaning within man's body as within a seed. The evolution of meaning in man, therefore, depends on his breath. His awareness, penetrated with the Spirit of Premeditation, is gradually brought to the radiant salt of meaning and neutralized in the marrow of his being. In this neutralized, preaware state, meaning reacts chemically as the responsive sculptor of man's physiological being.

Moved by the Spirit of Premeditation, which seeks its own self, awareness evolves to face its ancestor in the depth of its own existence. The memory of one divine self-creation is unsealing itself gradually, from its own scripture, which is the individual man. This memory, through many cycles of psychic evolution, traces the principle of existence to absorption. Man traverses many phases of psychic hunger until his awareness recognizes—within absorption itself—the substantiated form of inspiration.

Within the vortex of moving space and the spiral becoming of the stars, inspiration lives as potential breath. Within air it lives as potential eye and within stone as potential "I." Within the longing of existence, it lives as the potential "I am."

> For I have seen the abyss becoming I. He knew not the place in which I became, nor did he see me becoming his own face. [*Rev.* 10]

The Spiritual A Priori

Through the hermetic space of its individual wholeness or soul, which is the psyche, the Spirit of Premeditation gradually generates in man its own individualized awareness, or face. This new awareness, rising with man's evolution, is the revelation of man's soul, or wholeness, within the aware intellect. In becoming the reuniting synthesis between intuition and reason, intellect manifests as an ear-eye which defines its understanding, being an "I." This "I" is the awakening of measure within its space, which thus becomes the measurer. As a number in the infinity of the

One and a function in the universal harmony, intellect becomes the animator of the psychic space it occupies, the self-creator in his own abyss, the void. The "void" thus becomes aware of its own self as coherence, or soul. Thus the inertial space-time becomes the living "I," or Word of meaning.

This self-creative revelation in man of an intelligence which asserts itself differently from man's natural reasoning is the manifestation of the spiritual *a priori*. As the origin and content of all sacred books, it represents a bridge between nature-born rationality and man-born divine Word.

The spiritual a priori indirectly rules the *mental a priori* of space-time, which rules man's natural intelligence. In its direct revelation it behaves as the paradoxical, irrational, yet rationally formulated imperative of a new understanding: the rise to existence of meaning in man's intellect.

> I am the soul of Shu coming forth in the members of the one who creates himself from his own emanations. [*Rev.* 3]

Revelation

Intuition is manifested by the language of the emotions and is dependent on reason for its interpretation, while revelation asserts itself directly through reason, beyond interpretation or empirical cognition. Behind intuitive cognition stands nature. Thus intuitive intelligence represents a bond between man and nature, which all men feel and recognize. Behind revelation stands the Spirit of Premeditation. Although it does not relate to common experience, revelation always appears with clarity and precision. Intuition is the guardian of nature whereas revelation is the herald of nature's exaltation and is the ferment of transformations within the mind of man. Intuitive knowledge remains eternally equal to itself at all times and in all nations, but revelations alter. For as every hour of the day has its own light, so every stage in the evolution of awareness and every "time" in the evolution of humanity has its own *word* of exaltation. The more ancient the revelation, the more difficult it is for us to receive it in its original form. In the evolution of awareness a timely redefinition of the inconceivable "I" appears as a sacred word at the origin of all religions and philosophies. One could see such a redefinition as the mystical advent of a sudden mutation comparable to the creation of a new species. For a new species similarly represents the redefinition of a stage of the evolution of nature's preaware intelligence.

The primordial revelation is the principle behind coagulation. It is manifested in cosmic and natural life as a definition extracting itself as a visible "hill" from the ocean of its invisible self. Thus definition, as the force of revelation, is the origin of all contractive motion, physical or chemical, that causes dilation and manifests as a twofold function. This principle of contraction and dilation, the invisible mother-gland of life throughout cosmos and nature, is reflected in organic life as absorption and assimilation. This principle, by means of a complex network of interactions, results in man's capacity for verbal definition.

Intellect represents the animation of this capacity and reveals itself as the key quality of man's seed. Within intellect the Spirit of Premeditation manifests as the hidden definer of revelations. Standing behind the twofold root of nature, contraction and dilation, the Spirit of Premeditation also acts behind the twofold root of man's awareness, intuition and reason, through their uniter, intellect. This unity is manifested as the soul, the wholeness of man's individual life, and is reflected in its own hermetic space, the psyche. Using intuition as its force of understanding, the Spirit of Premeditation, seated as a nameless "I" within the intellect, draws to itself the knowledge of its existence, which it reveals to itself through its force of definition, reason.

> It is I who regenerate substance to restore the animator of the holy flesh of Osiris. [*Rev.* 16]

The Tropism of Reason

Following its hereditary, organic, and mental specification, reason, inseparable from awareness, issues subjective definitions. In its verbal articulation, reason acts indirectly as the antenna of intuition. At the same time it follows in its interpretation of life the individual codes of man's hereditary personality. Thus individuality arises *through* and not *from* subjectivity within the intelligence of creation as a mental specification and a judge. Reason, which may be compared to the activities of the physical seed, reveals this individuality as a hidden entity, the "I" inherent in the universe.

Regardless of the combinations of parental genes from which the specific nature of the physical existence of an individual is decided, and thus regardless of the orientation of its reason, organic individuality is the preaware thinker in man. Inscribed as a memory—an abstract seed—this thinker evolves as a potential bearer of the link between the natural "I" of man's awareness and the inconceivable "I." This link is manifested through awareness in which all trends of intelligence meet. As such, awareness, the fruit of the genesis of flesh, is the condition of the awakening in man of the *sleeping* ancestor, dormant in every life. This ancestor reveals himself through the evolution of synthetic intellect, the thinker, who manifests initially through reason, which is the intellect's force of definition.

Man's natural reason, however, as a mental faculty of organizing a priori concepts within a logical framework, is a form of tropism or responsive movement to an external stimulus. The very word "reflection," qualifying the act of reasoning, indicates its secondary and responsive nature.

Reason, in fact, reflects and automatically responds to an a priori, nonverbal structure of logic, in the same way as an animal instinctively responds to stimuli in its environment. Through reason, the structural codes of the universe and life are automatically reflected in man's verbal logic. Being the structurally deviated contractive force of soul (or wholeness), reason is the soul's force of coherence. But it is an unaware actor in all this. Its awareness is a stranger to soul, which is its true identity.

While man identifies and defines the codes of nature through reason, he identifies himself neither with these codes nor with reason, but only with his "I"—the "I" of intellect, the thinker who reasons. Yet this thinker, inseparable from reason, poses its reason as an eye through which, separated from its only observable origin, it naturally interprets life.

Thus, at the root of his intelligence, man is faced with a relationship between his individual awareness and preaware nature: a relationship that he can only define through a limited and conditioned form of intelligence, his reason.

One with preaware nature and its codes of behavior, reason gains its position as man's definer and judge only through the structural division at the base of the human brain, which in fact causes the relationship between preawareness and awareness, both of which are beyond the reach of reason.

I am the measure of heaven. [*Rev.* 33]

The Voluntary Harmonic Act

Turning inward and inquiring into the roots of his reason, man tumbles headfirst into the spiral abyss of his being, which suddenly seems to be the swallower of his reason. Although faced with this absurd negation of the supremacy of reason, man still believes that his reason is his dominant self. The certitude, beyond the empirical evidence, is the manifestation of the *positive absolute*. In the rural, intuitive man, this positive absolute is at the origin of his faith in the divine order. In the empirically minded rationalist, however, the positive absolute turns into the *negative absolute* of atheism. For while doubting everything, including divinity, reason never doubts itself.

It is hard for an empiricist to recognize that in reality he *feels* reason as his dominant self, although empirically he can only trace it to his brain cells. Through such recognition, however, reason can trace beyond empiricism the hidden "tonic" of its dominant self: a building intelligence (or "I") within its revolving night, which creates its own brain with all its cells. By sustaining the balance between this feeling and reason, intellect opens to its role of the harmonizer, aware of all the relationships among the constitutional parts of man.

This inner harmonization is comparable to *equal temperament* in music. Only through a harmonic system of equal temperament can the orchestra of man's constitutional parts yield harmony—the meaning of life. Like a prodigious musician, man's synthetic intellect creates harmonic meaning through a conceptual *correction* of the relativity data, by which it appears that individual functions of man's constitution clash, like the pitch of instruments in an untuned orchestra.

As the potential synthesis or harmonizer of all frequencies of intelligence, intellect seeks naturally to specify every pitch of truth in man. This is why it fosters analysis in the initial stages of its evolution. It is the sustainer of every aspect of relativity. By evolving as the analyzer, intellect cleaves to its rational power of elimination and radicalism. Analysis spreads the crown of its tree of reason. The wholeness of human nature is disjointed in that way, and capacities are orientated to become specialties. The force of elimination prunes it, seeking to control its expansion. These two dispositions of intellect grow in opposition to each other, like the sap in the tree and the gardener who seeks to prune it.

Through a tuning correction, synthetic intellect prunes man's turbulence. In this pruning act only disharmony is eliminated, not the individual value of each part of self-expression. The harmonic correction of the natural flow of understanding can only be completed by an order of wisdom comparable to the calendar. Within the calendar, a conceptual space—standing for time—is established through the equal temperament of the naturally unequal days and nights. Through this voluntary harmonic act, movement is revealed as a structure. *For only as a structure can it be grasped and canonized through a system of equal fractions, which defines time.*

Time, felt naturally as a shapeless flow into which man merges through the rhythm of his breath, is thus born as a concept of *measure* within the cosmic movement. This abstract birth of time in man, as a reflection and recognition of measure within the cosmic movement, brings human intelligence into the process of divine re-creation. This is why time was a "god" of intelligence in the past. The ancient world left its calendar to us and the seasonal worship of the time-god with it as a ritual commemoration of man's conceptual birth, the carnival.

Conceiving divinity through measure as intelligence, intellect embarrasses all religions and every form of science. Placed within the balance of a harmonic movement and not in space, such a concept of intelligence, although conceivable as the creator of life, cannot be represented directly by any imaginable form. Divinity springs forth in man as an "I" which recognizes itself as measure within movement.

I sum up my multiple shapes. [*Rev.* 18]

The Reintegration of Space and Time into Meaning

Meaning, behind preaware, instinctive, and aware life, be it universal, natural, or individual, constantly changes its aspects through the evolution of the qualities of its inconceivable intelligence. For as far as we can conceive creation, it reflects intelligence. We can trace intelligence through all perceptible frequencies and particles up to the boundary of space, which appears to us as void. Thus the "void" conceals the inconceivable conceiver that endlessly builds and destroys the galaxies, nature, and civilizations contained within it. It acts as a force of order from which both the universe and awareness stem. We can conceive the inconceivable conceiver within the void only if we recognize our own "I" as the inconceivable conceiver endlessly re-creating the substances of our net of life.

Within its timeless loom of intelligence, alone and changeless, the "I," alive in every sufferer, knits and unravels the stages of its timebound existence, in which it is the measurer of life and death. It permeates every speck of its universal being, orientating movement within all forms of energy and transmitting its spectrum of intelligence through space, air, fire, light, liquids, and solids. As an unobservable source of orientation at the base of all living beings, elements, and stars and of all contraction and expansion, it holds together its visible universe. In it, our aware "I," as its own inverted gaze, observes it from within. This living gaze does not belong to shapes and sizes—the contraction and expansion which reflect within it a graph of its own transformations—for it belongs to its inconceivable "I."

Beyond darkness and light, energy and matter, movement and stillness, preawareness, unawareness, and natural conceptual awareness, the universal "I" is the only knower. Encompassing through its Spirit of Premeditation all grades of knowing, generating, and extinguishing its prodigal force, it sustains its life-giving thought as breath sustains man. For breath alone, ungraspable as the bringer and taker of life, is akin to man's inconceivable "I."

Through breath, man enters into communion with the inexhaustible instant of universal life, experiencing it as *duration*. Although present, the instant, like duration, is untraceable. It never ends and thus cannot be conceived as having a beginning. Beyond quality, the instant into which he endlessly merges escapes judgment.

Through the instant, time appears as the presence in man of all-encompassingness: for beyond reason the instant is experienced as timeless duration of meaning conceiving time. By such experiences alone of time as an identity of one's own mind, timelessness may be conceived as an opposition to time.

Meaning contains time as the mother contains her childbearing womb, remaining unalterably whole throughout the stages of the fetal genesis of her child. Through time, meaning conceives its inconceivable self, manifesting its evolution through the principle of solidity—the invisible mountain. Time creates the weight of this mountain with its vegetation and life. Its peak is intellect. Through intellect time can grasp its own instant as spaceless timelessness, and, merging with it, conceive itself as the intelligence of meaning.

The understanding of intelligence, which lives in man as the pacemaker lives in his heart, is not natural to him, although it is through this hidden pacemaker that he lives and dies. For beyond his awareness, limited by the natural a priori as space-time, his hidden "I" of meaning belongs to its inconceivable self, which traverses space and time, death and decomposition, fermentation and corruption, and moves the atmospheric fusion of evaporating gases and fumes which rise from earth and sink into it again. It dwells in animals, plants, all reactive, unaware tropisms, and within all human cells, as a receiving and emitting end among all parts of its creation. It permeates all genetic particles and all dust traveling between stars. As it breathes in and out, its inexhaustible Spirit of Premeditation creates and re-creates the worlds, building and destroying its own revelations within the ocean of its own breath.

> I rule those who rule fatality. I realize the realizer. I sustain the sustainer. I destroy the destroyer, for I abominate destruction. [*Rev.* 32]

The Imperishable Salt of Meaning

While the steady spiral flow of the universal life inertially obeys the great seasons of its natural rise and fall, it also shelters, like a huge vat, a permanent, invisible movement of distillation. This invisible movement beyond size and shape and in all substances manifests the Spirit of Premeditation, which shapes its conceptual evolution as the physical gene molds its flesh. It is the weaving of the hidden weaver, the dream of the sleeping ancestor, and the potency of the potential prince of resurrection.

Captured in all creation, the spirit animates and sustains as the specified salt of meaning at the core of life, all seed and all natural laws. Subtle and empirically undetectable, this subtle salt acts as the preaware "I" in the organic life. It is the moving egg of the "phoenix" eternally rising from the ashes and traversing species as the essence of the natural evolution. Manifold and sole, meaning permeates all creatures at the core of their existence. It beams from within their bodies and sustains their genetic codes.

In man, the Imperishable Salt of Meaning from within his

marrow reactively rules his existence. It is "This" which hears and "understands" the language of the sun and stars and reacts to it accordingly to its memory, or seed, of that man. It thus defines reactively his life span. Within the network of universal existence, galaxies and planets are born and die within the limit of the same vital definition to which man's life is subjected.

Premeditation substantiates its own self, according to its life-giving spirit, the origin at the core of all substance. Through the rise of species it causes the evolution of awareness to reach the individual as an entity, the natural "I." This entity, the natural "I," is placed like a king within his own planet which has given him life. His awareness, manifesting the radiance of meaning, is the harmonic bond between meaning and life. As such, it is a potency which can ensure the balance and regeneration of all perishable existence within the imperishable loom of meaning, sustaining its own essence amid the swarm of perishable stars. Like a cloth with its endless patterns, this swarm of stars and constellations flows, inspiring its appointed "breath" within its appointed time. The weaver, within its imperishable loom, the inconceivable "I," eternally re-creates the perishable cradle which holds death as an ever-crying infant whose heart is forged into an imperishable eye.

The forging of this radiant eye of meaning, as the sustainer of the universe and the origin of the Word through which the preaware premeditation is becoming aware, takes place in man. Man's natural awareness is a closed eye of meaning, born as a condition of its own opening to its own inner, inconceivable "I." Through human awareness, the Word of meaning reaches the meaning of which it is the Word.

> It is I who create the monster of destruc-
> tion. The scorching blast of her jaws is
> not turned against me. It is I who ferry the
> monster, creating her scepter in the
> midst of her destroyers. [*Rev.* 27]

Meaning

The origin of the absolute order which rules the universe is meaning, seated at its core and permeating every speck of existence, like an invisible octopus spreading its tentacles. The "tentacles" are the root functions, creating and ruling their galactic flesh. However huge and complex or small and simple, organic or inorganic, matter or mind, existence behaves as one indivisible flesh. Every part relates to the whole, the "octopus," which moves in all directions, at all times, as the unchangeable "I am," in its manifestation of the law of causes and consequences.

The perfect, living mechanism by which planets orbit around the sun and never collide is also the force of fatality which causes the rage of cataclysms and the ruin of civiliza-tions. We all know that the life-sustaining water and the floodwater which swallows villages with their populations and cattle, are the "same" water. But we do not recognize this "sameness" in the opposite behavior of the creative energy within man himself.

Meaning rules creation and its cycles, self-ordained and unchangeable throughout the diversity of its worlds. It traverses destruction, fire, and earthquake, the death of galaxies and suns, specifying its spirit, within which it conceives itself as the "I am."

The "pagan" world knew this. We have forgotten it at a high price. They had a structure of "gods," the blind per-petuators of existence, monsters and dragons which could not, however, harm the "dweller within creation." They conceived the order within time and its cycles through "decans," the basic unit of ten, composed of primary numbers. These "numbers" were the root functions of the universal measure within its inertial movement, specified through the "word" of their transitory meaning, the decan. Sacred geometry at the base of temples was the geometry of organs, within the house of meaning, which was man. Specified as the subtle salt, meaning was conceived as the mover of the genetic alteration of seeds and the cross-pollination which manifests itself through the evolution of nature. Their worship of "gods" was man's worship of the ecological whole and thus of self-sustenance.

We have rendered ourselves unable to discern between the blind forces of nature and the principles involved in the genesis of an aware system of balance, the animate, individual measurer of the inertial movement in the mind. In that way, the attention of the human being has been turned away from responsibility to the existence of meaning of such words as "good," "evil," "prosperity," "freedom," and "love." The "good" disappears. God is to blame. God disappears, too. Ignorance remains to fashion the heart of man, following the blind "gods" of creation reflected in his desires. Being the reflections of the root functions which rule the "logic" of causes and consequences, they foster misconception in man as a logical self-conception of the "I," within the net of its unfathomable self.

Like the brain, with all its circumvolutions of preaware and aware life, creation is an inherent part of the inconceivable "I," the meaning. Through creation or preaware thought meaning forges its aware words, while being itself indefinable by any standard of our reason, including the concept of awareness itself. Although, through the absolute order of its specification, existence unchangeably follows its cycles of creation and destruction, self-conception of meaning, situated in man's awareness, is destined to rise above creation.

The *Word*, born of man, is mediator between the inconceivable "I," its pure Spirit of Premeditation, and premeditation itself, which *is* existence. Stepping out from space and time, the aware *Word* is still one with it (that is, space-time) just as the natural human awareness is a step away from the animal yet still one with it and able to communicate with it.

Meaning awakening from creation is like the seed dropping from its tree. Although it is a new kernel, this seed is one with the original seed of the tree. The tree itself is nothing but the seed in its self-reproductive genesis. In a similar way, the individual awareness awakening from its tree, which is both the physical body and nature herself, is one with the inconceivable "I" at the origin of nature.

The elaboration and enthronement of a new synthesis among all fields of intuitive and empirical cognition act as the hidden sustainer of morality and order in today's world, which suffers from the lack of understanding of its harmonic imperative. From the want of vital information concerning that imperative, humanity has gained wrong ideas about the most important issues of human life, such as freedom, good and evil, prosperity, failure, and especially, love. For instance, God is qualified as "good." The consequence of this qualification is logical: if God is almighty and good, then why is there so much evil?

Without an understanding, enshrined at the base of a civilization, of the harmonic essence of the bond between the tree of existence and its divine seed, there can be no true faith. Without true faith there can be no true conception of order and no sound reason for morality. Without order and morality human life is doomed to self-destruction. Disorder and immorality become destroyers, and, coming from within, they destroy man himself, their conceiver.

I have forged my soul which gave me birth, for older than its revelation am I, the Knower. [*Rev.* 21]

PART II

The Somersault of Awareness

O gods, your mind does not evolve through your own utterance, but through me alone. My becoming is the force of the entire creation, which flows forth from the Word of the great Lord "This." [*Rev.* 28]

CHAPTER 4

The Dark Sanctuary of Soul

My soul does not honor the gods of
magical spells, those circular lords of
eternity. [Rev. 35]

The Body of Coherence

In man, absorption is the eternal, contractive "I want"
(hunger) while assimilation manifests as its evolving "I am"
(self-cognition). As natural forms are annihilated in a process of mechanical hacking and chemical dissolution and
offered as a sacrifice to assimilation, so in man's mind
experiences are digested and assimilated according to his
psychic hunger. As a mental force of desire, absorption
generates indiscriminate consumption, egotism, disorder,
and pain, yet as a tentacle of soul, it is also a building force
in man. In man's intellect, psychic hunger acts as the selective force of self-assessment, which manifests itself through
absorption yet belongs to assimilation.

As we trace assimilation through the different realms, we
can see it acting through an increasingly complex network
of specified reactions. From the monosystem of mineral
chemistry, it evolves into the binary (absorption-as-
similation) principle of the vegetable realm. The root, as an
absorbing tentacle, is the builder of the network of its
substantiation. In the animal realms it becomes a centralized system of instinctive consciousness which, through
innate patterns of behavior, commands hunt, defense, and
self-perpetuation. Then, in man, all dimensions of assimilation meet: the mineral in the bone and the blood, the
vegetable in the tree of metabolic circuits, and the animal in
the flesh. Assimilation is the force of coherence or *soul*
which, as an abstract body, holds all these moving circuits
within itself. *Soul, within all seed, holds together all parts of its
wholeness.*

As container and womb of all seed-born genesis, soul is
the origin of the magnetism holding together the separated

parts of the inconceivable, original whole. Every seed in nature may be seen, beyond its primary shape, as an abstract whole, substantiating its coherence by the gradual evolution of an aware, individual *system of balance*, based on a preliminary generation of its parts. Thus every being which evolves from its seed is both a constant separation from and a constant reunion with the abstract whole, incarnated in its own seed.

The world, with all its individual life forms belonging to their individual seeds, reveals a soul of its own, which it manifests in all its complexity. The spirit of an age is the seeker of soul, acting through this soul's own force of assimilation in individual and group behavior.

We could say that the separation of man's awareness from his organic and instinctive intelligence is a structural framework which may only be understood as a door with a double lock. For man's higher, abstract intelligence can be activated as a mutant of his own mind only if he understands the mental division in himself as a manifestation of the relationship between the two creative streams which are the root of all life: *inertial movement and animate intelligence*.

> My soul does not serve the gods who work the net for catching souls. My soul does not honor the gods of magical spells, those circular lords of eternity. [*Rev.* 35]

The Animate System of Balance

Inertial movement and intelligence appear out of the night of time as the two poles of the ungraspable oneness behind the graspable fragmentation of phenomena and laws. For inertial movement, as the inanimate perpetuator of planetary orbits and of the net of the reactivities of physical and chemical laws, can be recognized in every aspect of observable living substance, as a tropism. But the animate mover, similarly, can be recognized in every aspect of inanimate motion.

Inertia seems to rule all living cycles. It is the wheel of life which ordains the ceaseless dance or behavior of all animate or inanimate forms—"dancers" rising like shadows and falling to dust. But within these "shadows" rising from the wheel of life, intelligence generates the perpetual creative balance between life and death, existence and nonexistence, being and nonbeing within all substance. It is an active crossing point and an axis, holding together all functions of the unstoppable movement, which is the "dance" in its mystical space, time itself.

> Glorifying Ra-Atum, I exalt Nu. It is I who regenerate substance to restore the animator of the holy flesh of Osiris.
> [*Rev.* 16]

The Mover of Genesis and Time

Inertial movement is, as it were, the "echo" of the generative "voice" which is the seminal quality of the Spirit of Premeditation rising in the premeditation or seed. It is the inanimate force of cohesion (soul). Intelligence manifests itself as the hidden mover of the stages of expansion of the seminal pattern, creating time, which thus carries the evolving scripture of the seed of premeditation. In this way, time comes into existence through inertia as mystical space of seminal expansion.

Inertial movement comes into existence reactively from the generative impulse of the separation of the oneness of the seed (or premeditation). It continues this movement, manifesting the seminal intelligence for the creation of the functional parts of a new whole: the evolving system of balance. These parts, in their creation, tend to separate from their origin, the abstract whole, that is, the *system of balance*. Thus inertia manifests itself as a twofold force: *resistance* to the seminal intelligence and the infinite *sustenance* and continuation of the engendered movement. Wholeness, or soul, in the seed resists fragmentation by pulling together its separated parts and thus generates the irresistible force of resistance to fragmentation within all created forms. But, at the same time, as the cohesion of the indivisible and the infinite, it lives in every separated "part" of the whole or seed as the sustainer of its inherent spirit. In this way it acts as the sustainer of all movement generated by the Spirit of Premeditation, the mover in the seed. This sustaining force of inertia generates "egotism," the "I" of each created part.

The twofold aspect of inertia, resistance and sustenance, is thus generated by the premeditated splitting of the whole seed and the gathering of its structured parts. Space emerges from premeditation as an a priori framework—the time-space of the intelligence of creation. This time-space is the womb and creative loom of the Spirit of Premeditation in its continuous seminal act.

Within time-space, inertia is the soul's force. As it obeys and thus sustains the original creative impulse of the Spirit of Premeditation, it realizes the premeditated creative movement, but within this creative movement and its created phenomena, the inherent *spirit* is active, as the mover of its ensuing transformations. The premeditation, or Word, thus becomes living existence.

Reacting to inertia as a restrictive and active balance and shaping and moving its relationships, *animate intelligence* manifests the spirit within the force of its premeditation. This is why intellect impregnated by rationality acts at a certain stage of its evolution as a reactive power, the irra-

tional attacker of nature. The origin of this aggressive attitude lies, strangely, in the shaping quality of the seed.

The seed as an abstract whole has no quality or quantity.
Its manifestation is the rise of its shaping spirit. Inertia and
its movement of creation are originated in the impulse that
results from the awakening of this shaping within the vir-
ginal seed.

In man's psyche, inertia manifests through rationality.
Intuition, on the other hand, is the manifestation of the
animate coherence of the shaping quality (or spirit) of the
seed. The relationship of intellect to rationality, its inanimate carrier expressing the force of cohesion or inertia,
and to intuition, is the living system of balance within the
cross of existence. The cross is infinite sacrificial opposition
and the balance rising within it is the coherence of its
oneness.

This animate system of balance between cohesion and
coherence is the only stable element in creation—the shaper in the void hooking motion to its original life-giving
thought. The expansive tendency of inertia is dominated by
the restrictive intelligence of the seed. Through this continuous shaping act of a seminal intelligence, inertial movement sustains order in the universe.

> I forge my soul in creating the concept of
> my soul within the dwellers of the Lake of
> Fire. [*Rev.* 22]

The Balance

In man, too, the reactive motion of organic and psychic
behavior obeys the system of balance of the shaping, preaware intelligence of his seed. This shaping intelligence,
which reconceives man continuously at each instant of his
organic life, manifests at each instant of his natural life as

the preaware, active balance of two unequal dimensions: *reason* and *intuition*. When this shaping intelligence penetrates man's awareness, it becomes an unnatural, conceptual entity, the eye of meaning. The relationship between this unnatural "eye" and the natural intelligence in man is the edification in him of a life different from his natural life, the life of meaning.

> By such *seeing*, I surge from the Mysterious Shrine as he who creates himself. [*Rev.* 31]

The Measurer

Man generates philosophical existence within himself. Because every new step in his search for truth is a wall erected between nature and himself, this evolution builds a labyrinth in him. Becoming aware of inner complexity, man creates and re-creates abstract, autonomous concepts, seeking a definition for each. His own rationality, as a manifestation of the law of cause and consequence, responds to these like a hydra-headed dragon. It grows opposite yet interrelated and autonomous heads for each. By this means man enters into a relationship with a *measurer* in himself, rising from the disturbed natural balance between weight (reason) and measure (intuition).

This measurer rises as a new conceptual "I," the owner of the unnatural *eye*, emerging in his natural "I," the psyche. Having lost the wholeness of its natural identity, the "I" finds itself as a living naught or nothing within the infinite number, or a fragmentation of its own torn whole now become a nullity. Only by conceiving the abstract principle of a system of balance as the oneness of the fragmented parts of its own self can the measurer conceive meaning itself. This conception is the generation of meaning within its own existence.

While inertia, like an avalanche, perpetuates and amplifies the reactive determinism of perishable existence based on balance, meaning, sunk like a seed in the balance of its foundations, inwardly opens its two arms from its weightless center, the conceptual "I." It is the measurer, rising from the measure (intuition) and thus creating a split between weight (reason) and the imperturbable master of measure (the Spirit of Premeditation). By this split, the omnipotent law of cause and consequence by which the balance was disturbed is overridden by the lightning flash of the law-giver, the spirit within its own premeditation.

The revelation of meaning within its own inert carrier may be seen as the mystical, abstract origin of all genesis. It is present in the blind striving of the worm, as a ceaseless plowing; it is present in the opaque earth, as the opening of its scale of precious metals and its rainbow of gemstones; it is present in man, as the rise of something comparable to a new primary color.

> I am the one great in mastery of the functions of his vessel. My strength and potency are greater than all powers. [*Rev. 8*]

The Contractive Principle of Soul

While meaning, in its slow revelation, evolves through the opening of its own conceptual eye, this very opening in its essence is manifested, paradoxically, as a *contractive principle*.

Within matter this contractive principle is both the creator of forms and the breaking force of death. Within mind it is both a pool of fire, egotism, which swells, threatening life, and the dweller in his fiery pool. Within creation it is the principle of the network which perpetuates itself as the shaping constraint ever evolving beyond its own ceaseless transformations.

The soul's contractive principle is at once the potter of shapes and the measurer of the extent of the destructive force through which the inconceivable "I" shapes and reshapes its moving, living net. It may be identified with the principle of physical existence, for it substantiates every form of density.

The totality of celestial bodies appears to be still. Yet in its essence the still, starry sky is a moving pattern of fixed relationships in which the earth itself is included. This fixed pattern of movement cannot be separated from the preaware intelligence of its cosmic balance. As the perpetuator of a balance of fixed relationships between the individual and cosmic bodies, this intelligence is a fiery, moving flow that acts as a shaping constraint.

Elementary creation, as a structure inseparable from its movement and propagating itself through its endless cycles of unknown yet law-abiding balance, perpetually recreates its elements and circuits within a single flow. This flow constantly falls back upon itself in a self-consuming turmoil which behaves like clay within the constraint of a potter's wheel. Constraint, like the potter's hands, shapes this inert flow, rolling huge solitary boulders across the sky. Planets, stars, solar systems, and galaxies obey the laws of their own existence, yet all are subject to a single moving balance which is at once constraint and structure.

Every network is a form of constraint. The constant interrelationships, however complex, of the moving swarm of celestial bodies indicate a single flow of expanding constraint. This constant balance within the moving network of related heavenly bodies, in its inconceivable space, traces invisible shapes and volumes, like a concealed graph or memory. These are components of an immaterial scripture, the testimony of preaware thought present in its elementary self.

Although perpetuated through movement, preaware thought is stillness, moving the cosmos. Within this seed-like "stillness" of its self-perpetuating movement, a potential change dwells as a premeditation. This premeditation is the potential thinker, a new, evolutionary dimension rising from the elementary structure of the preaware thought. Creation may thus be conceived as one self-perpetuating seed. Evolution is its germination. The universe is one with its inconsumable preaware thought, which it inertly perpetuates; the evolution of organic life appears both as a separation from it and as the potential revelation of the thinker. The process of this germination is therefore the *evolution of nature's structural principle into an aware structure of intelligence: man.*

> I forge my soul in creating the concept of my soul within the dwellers of the Lake of Fire. Thus I conceive myself through the gods, whom I carry as my crown.
> [*Rev.* 22]

The Defining Principle of Soul

In man, the uniformity of instinctive reactions is broken down to definite concepts and ideas. Man evolves beyond nature by identifying, not with nature herself, but with his own definitions of nature, which slowly evolve to become a barrier between him and his natural origin.

Through the symmetry of unequal qualities of human perception, the principles of creation are singled out from their natural oneness with phenomena and reconnected to each other, as a network of brain functions forming determined perceptual fields. Through this a priori network, mental perceptions are led into a maze of connections and disconnections, and words surge forth as transitory revelations of the synthesis of these interrelations.

It could be said that mental coherence, like life itself, is the presence of the whole in the relations arising from a proportional division of this inconceivable whole into unequal but complementary parts. This division itself is the germination of a proportionally growing definition of the whole, reflected within the network of its dissolution.

Thus life in its evolution both *solidifies* its abstract, *life-giving thought* by creating its net of articulate organisms and *dissolves* it through perpetual fragmentation. By such a process of simultaneous solidification and dissolution, its *evolving intelligence prepares the functional base for the great reversal of the initial process of the concretion of thought into its organism. In this reversal the organic structures of nature are converted, through man, into the functions of aware thought.*

> Inconceivable to the gods of creation, he edifies his name. [*Rev.* 12]

The Root of the Principle of Definition

The continuous rise of life from "stillness," perpetuated by the inertial movement of its interconnected heavenly systems, can only be due to a particular inherent *condition* by which the potential change within this stillness, or seed, is activated in a part of its cosmic structure. From this point of view, the solar system is a specific "ganglion" of moving forces, a *root* carrying in its very constitution the blueprint of changes. Through these changes the spirit of premeditation, which generates life, manifests itself.

Although the rise and evolution of life are comparable to a tree growing from a seed, this "seed," the universe, does not destroy itself germinating as it does in nature but, while evolving its "tree," stays unchanged, perpetuating its own structure as through a permanently active root condition and basis for the continuous regeneration of life. Thus, although universal creation as the foundation of organic life seems to precede life, it remains timelessly present within the passing time of the rise and fall of its self-regenerative cycles.

The moving pattern of fixed celestial relationships is the self-reproductive memory and testimony of preaware thought, which is the preconceiver of life, its revelation. Life slowly awakens to its memory of life-giving thought to reveal itself to itself. Beyond the "solid" state of a structured universe, the inscribed celestial relationships of patterns (the memory) contain its captured Spirit of Premeditation, which, imperishable and beyond quantity, manifests itself continuously through the successive cycles of revelations of its meaning.

Preaware meaning cannot be separated from its unaware manifestation, which is the physical universe, just as natural awareness cannot separate itself from its organic animator, man's body. The evolution of awareness is the evolving *memory* of life-giving, structural transformations, inscribed in his seed. Through this memory a new, unnatural evolving system of balance (or measure) creates itself, shaping the birth of the revelation of the seed's integral memory. In this vital revelation, awareness becomes the living name (Word) of the Spirit of Premeditation and Word of meaning.

I have drawn onto my head the weaver's crown. [*Rev.* 30]

The Organic Net and the
Architectural Meaning of Desire

Each organic seed, however primitive, is a net in which cosmic energy is snared and structurally channeled into a pattern of individual behavior. This "snare" acts as an inconceivable form of intelligence, giving rise to specific organisms with innate patterns of behavior. The degree of dexterity and ingenuity in these patterns results from variations of structural organization within the snare or net. The evolutionary steps of the creation of species are due to unobservable acts of reorientation, traced in the patterns trapped in the seed. These cause the qualitative changes which are the moving components of the one evolving intelligence, and reveal an unknown form of *tropism* which obeys, beyond light and chemistry, the undeservable, *architectural meaning* of life-giving, preaware thought.

This preaware thought, closer to a shaping desire than to reason, is the sleeping architect who builds his body in a dream from which he rises as a phantom, taking possession of this body in the name of awareness. Like Jonah resting in the whale, this partial, natural awareness is still a dream within the sleeping architect. As dream and reality differ from us, so the preaware, genetic codes and awareness are two different states of one intelligence. We are often tempted to read a human type of intelligence in animals, or even to see man as a "degree" of animality. But although there is some truth in both assessments, they represent the vain effort of human natural reason to reduce all life to its own limited "measure." The "sameness" for which all men yearn cannot be found in the physical world, which is based on inequality, but is found only in the constant proportional balance that manifests *through* inequality.

At the core of all life, whether in the cosmos, nature, or man, we find the proportional net of balance manifesting as an abstract vessel of transformations. This net can be seen as the "holy mother" or as the mythical whale. It may be felt as the soul, or as an all-devouring monster into which all sinks and from which all rises only to sink again, or as a common dark mother who gives birth and annihilates and draws light into her lightless womb. Like death itself, she is the lever of transformations, and a door to an unknown dimension. One may recognize this principle of womb or vessel in the structure of the mineral or in the atmosphere itself. One may also discover it in all creatures as the generative "space" trapped by the valves, tubes, ducts, and tunnels of flesh. For the all-containing net of balance is not a physical container but that through which all physical containers act. It is this inconceivable "I" which snares itself within its net as the potential dweller.

In the vessel of the earth's atmosphere, organic life is a moving net of fixed relationships: a self-reproductive egg creating its premeditated chick, as a condition through which its aware thinker may rise to existence.

> Strong and powerful, it is I who am the origin of all gods. For I reinstate the word of the ancestor of all creation as the begetter of his own *generations*, which will perform my evolution through the ocean of time. [*Rev.* 9]

The Mutant Face

The animal realm, like the fruit, represents *mobility*—that is, a detachment of an evolved structure from its fixed root. Man, however, transcends mobility by fixing the root of nature, the principle of intelligence, in his head. Through his awareness he exalts in his head the three phases of transformation embodied in the head of a plant. The plant is at first a blossom, then a fruit, finally a seed. Through his awareness the principle of intelligence grows its own successive plants in man. Each plant, or mental phase, generates the following plant. Their succession thus forms a chain, each link being a complete cycle. Intelligence moves through this succession, drawing to itself what belongs to its evolution. This abstract, conceptual intelligence is *spirit*, individualized in man, extracting itself from its premeditation, which *is* man. In its manifestation it could be visualized as a blossom, in its transformations through mental pain and separation from nature as one huge fruit, and in its radiance as seed.

As man passes through the successive phases of the development of the plant in the evolution of his awareness his mind connects the phases of this vegetative evolution in one mental simultaneity which is the womb of the evolution of his abstract intelligence.

Within man's mental being, this simultaneity represents a structural mutation of nature. Man's intellect grows, like the plant's head, in chronological phases. First it blooms; then, as a mature fruit, it becomes "detached" from the organic structure of its bearer. Finally, like the seed, it is the synthesis resulting from this life. Yet whereas the seed of the plant can only generate another plant, man's conceptual intelligence, as a mental synthesis resulting from a process of maturation, returns upon itself to act as the mutator of its own root.

In the human physical seed, nature's evolution is concluded. Through the evolution of conceptual intellect, this seed, like a grafted fruit tree, indirectly generates a new, unnatural life in man—a life of meaning.

Meaning, as the hidden ruler of the evolution of the individual intellect, springs to existence through the natural principle of the self-perpetuation of the species, the reproductive seed. Bypassing the natural chain of individual birth and death, meaning manifests itself as a universal, *concealed head* revealing its individual face through man's conceptual evolution. In man's individual head, meaning acts as the mutator of the root of nature, duality.

In man, nature meets her challenger. Emerging from his natural seed as a phenomenon bound to all natural laws, man is the premeditated mutator of nature. Within this premeditated challenge, the individual performs his intellective evolution unknowingly, rising as a second self, the divine shadow, from the dark sanctuary of his soul.

Through man, life-giving thought reproduces its inconceivable self indirectly. Awareness, alone in unaware nature, rising as a seeking head, meets the preaware *ancestor* who claims it as his own birth. For man's genesis in nature is the genesis of the awareness of nature's preaware thought as it searches for its ancestral head.

In ever-widening waves of organic propagation, this *search* (evolution) sinking into its own infinity, spreads the life-giving kernel of its potential conclusion. From its depths it reemerges as an ever-changing watchman, raising its transitory faces, or revelations, above the whirlpool of its self-creation.

These transitory faces, marking the steps of the ancestor's self-assessment, are the defined species in nature and the phases of intellective evolution in man. Thus, like a blind weaver, life-giving thought reproduces its inconceivable self by first creating the warp and woof of the reproductive, physical seeds of its conceptional definitions.

Through these it subsequently acts as both the seeking root and the mutant. The history of man in nature is the interdimensional chronology through which the evolution of the awareness of the life-giving thought traces its invisible steps in the stream of its natural propagation. Through man life-giving thought creates its own self-devouring, self-re-creating, mutant face.

I regenerate the offering to restore the *animator* of the divine flesh. I come forth in the flesh of the Lord "This" to restore his being and reveal the sky as a full bloom—the oneness which sums up all creative laws. [*Rev.* 17]

The Devourer and the Offering

In nature, from its dark sanctuary of earth, the mineral realm sustains the vegetable realm, and the vegetable realm exalts, in the mobile animal, the paths of its transformations. In man, the vegetable realm (his metabolism), performing transformation beyond his mental control, is stimulated by a *psychic hunger*, resulting from rationalized animal drives. Although felt as an emotional impulse, psychic hunger, or *desire*, is rationally based, as it expressed man's spontaneous *interpretation* of the relationship between the world felt as exterior to him and his instinctive, emotional drives.

In man, animal drives become passions, desire, and mental cravings. Seated in the depth of his organs, these drives act in the psyche where they perform a double role: they feed the human being and they eat him. Although hunger feeds man, it can also kill him. As a mental network, man represents an obstacle to the natural order by which animals, moving like sap in the preaware peace of sleep and the hunt, uninhibitedly tread their predestined paths. In man this pure animal has been slaughtered, eaten, digested, and assimilated into a trigger at the base of his mind which is activated by its animate ghost, the psychic hunger.

Strangely enough, through reason, emerging with man, a beheaded, disorderly animal realm is placed in the position of directing the quality and efficiency of the vegetative transformations (metabolism) which provide the necessary sustenance for the stability of the mineral realm. The mineral balance of the whole body, of the bone and the subtle metabolism of the marrow and blood, is reflected in man's mental balance. Thus man's capital quality, his mental coherence, depends indirectly on the orientation of his psychic hunger, which, as the basis of his emotional life, will accordingly sustain or demolish him.

One with bone, the sustainer of his blood and the omnipotent lord of his transformations, man's intellect seated in his mental balance is an invisible mineral, self-created and older than birth. Yet moved by the hidden logic of its insatiable psychic hunger, intellect indiscriminately consumes its own base, like time itself. This paradoxical self-devouring conceiver is the root both of man's capacity to overcome nature and of his tragic inability to do so. It bears the impression, like a testimonial seal, of the ratio between psychic hunger and the revelation of life-giving thought that is man's hidden "I." This "seal" is a premeditated condition for a reversal, structurally conceived and physically concealed, of the relationship found in nature between inertia and animate intelligence.

Ruled by traditional codes of behavior which maintain the natural balance of inertia and intelligence, man remains unaware of the seed of reversal concealed in his head. This dangerous condition, however, only becomes apparent after the breakdown of tribal and rural societies. As a consequence of the development of urban industrial society and its accompanying technological mentality, man, separated from the fixed hierarchies of natural life, becomes a new, tribeless type of nomad, living on his own confused, individual wits. In the proportion that his intellect develops, his "hunger" for individual affirmation becomes more and more difficult to satisfy, and natural, healthy animal drives and appetites degenerate into mental cravings and new, unnatural needs.

Thus the natural order by which mineral sustains plant and plant sustains animal is reversed in man. The stream of his evolving intelligence begins, like a diver, to fathom its unknown depths. Sinking into the profundity of his roots, man lowers his awareness into his preaware self. Man's awareness thus grows through his descent.

This descent leads man to penetrate, directly or indirectly, into the depths of his own awareness. Like a weight which is also the harpoon thrown by his hidden "I," psychic hunger draws man toward its source. Thereby man recognizes the double movement, the living balance, of which he is a part. For within the weight, which is himself, a new weight conterbalances his descent by rising. This rising weight emerges as "the measurer" of depth, against which intellect grows into self-cognition. Thus, in man's intellect a synthesis comes gradually into existence which both specifies the weights of an abstract, vital balance and, like a plummet, shows whether the base of the balance is level. This synthesis is the cornerstone of his intellective self-edification. It points to a higher judge within him who, perceived as a devourer who indiscriminately swallows dreams, arguments, and theories, is really the hunger for the absolute truth: the hidden regenerator of the offering.

Psychic hunger is an enigmatic mediator which, like the sphinx itself, guards something invisible to man—his soul. It is the soul's hidden emissary, supporting the principle of *vital cohesion* by fostering indirectly the evolution of mental *coherence*. Its force, desire, is the threefold source of man's need to breathe, consume, and think. Like a fiery root or ratio in the earth, psychic hunger seeks the measure of water which it must draw from the atmosphere.

Thus man reasons, eats, and loves, not according to his apparent mental preference, but according to this hunger. As the undivided source of his reactions, this hunger represents the only natural, true uniter of his being. Consuming his hunger he becomes once more one ageless whole. Through this hunger, his intellect, as the ruler of man's assimilative orientation, indirectly defines his need at any given moment and moves his whole being by that definition. This synthesis marks the assimilative steps of the self-cognition of nature's concealed head.

I rule those who rule fatality. [*Rev.* 32]

The Force of Desire

Psychic hunger could be visualized in the form of a pendulum swaying on its axis, which is the right angle. The farther the pendulum swings to one side, the stronger is the pull to the other. When the pendulum comes to rest, it becomes the plumb line. Thus one could say that the force which moves the pendulum is that of the potential plumb line, moving reactively according to the distance from the right angle, its equilibrium. This distance dictates the quality and intensity of the psychic hunger through which man's individual balance seeks its right angle. Yet unlike its geometrical symbol, this "right angle" of mind is not a standard measure or moral precept. For each person it is an individual *missing segment* to be found and fitted into the ball of life: a harmonic keystone of mental coherence to be interlocked with the edifice of life-giving thought. Within this edifice each individual intellect finds its specific harmonic exaltation as the son of man—the species—or, in other words, as a resurrection of the precreational whole— the ancestor.

Man does not, like realms or species, embody a limited aspect or stage of creation. He represents both the negation of such limited stages and their synthesis. Containing all realms and species as functional parts of his mental being, man summarizes all realms in a continuous process of assimilation. By this all natural aspects of absorption and assimilation are converted into a single individual awareness.

The human psyche, the natural "I," one with its "eye" (intellect), emerges as the aware and preconceived effect of the preaware synthesis of all natural realms. Through psyche, the key quality of the evolution, individual reason, is brought naturally, as an aware force of coherence, to orientate the process of assimilation to which it owes its existence but which it does not understand. Although intellect is the assimilative "I" of intellection and aware judgment or choice, it functions through reason and within the framework of absorption. Absorption, in its turn, operates through psychic hunger, which psyche feels as its emotional identity.

In this way, although identified to man and aware of its functional self in relation to the exterior world, intellect is naturally unaware of its preaware self—the spirit—rising from the fruit of its premeditation which is man. As the ever-evolving, conceptual thinker behind both absorption and assimilation in man, intellect cannot be defined as solely rational, but rather must be defined as the moving center of balance in human awareness of its rational and its intuitive intelligence.

Aware of itself as a conceptual separation from what surrounds it, intellect establishes a scale of philosophical values according to its mental drives and needs. *Yet these needs spring from its reason's interpretation of the paradoxical relationship between the world in itself and its own force of definition (the very same reason) through which intellect manifests its own conceptual separation from the world.* However, this exterior world, as an apparent nonself with all its "other" lives, is also what intellect belongs to. This *belonging* is the hidden bond, a ratio ruling all levels of man's existence. It reveals itself in the preaware hunger for conceptual reunion. Aware intellect interprets this preaware hunger according to the rational framework of its hereditary and social circumstances. Aggression, idealism, pessimism, optimism, ambition, and purposelessness are thus but the varying shadows of man's insatiable hunger for love. Registering his separation from that which he belongs to, man feels a tremor close to pain at the root of his existence. This tremor of the birth of solitude, which links his hunger to his mind, is a trigger of the inner hunter whose prey, alas, is man's own ever-changing shadow.

> I shall rise to power in them, from within, to give him [the ancestor] the redeemer of his body through my genesis. [*Rev.* 9]

The Tail-Eater

Leaving the warm, watery womb, man confronts the cold immensity of the air, facing the earth upside down like a diver. From that instant on, he seeks his lost oneness with space and time, of which the only relic is his pulse. As a separation, he evolves around his pulse. His mind emerges from it, in constant spasm and pursuit, like a dancer. He is a tail in search of its head and a head in search of its tail.

Physically, as a tail, man surges from the spiral of his womb-life and grows spirally around himself, creating his self-sustaining and self-devouring net. Mentally, as a head, he surges from this net and faces himself as the self-sustaining and self-devouring spiral. His natural "I" is the bearer of this dramatic relationship, which both conceals and reveals his inconceivable "I." One with sea, sand, rock, and crevice, this inconceivable "I," nature's sleeping king, rises in man to confront the immensity of his self-creation. Surrounded by his own emanations, as in a womb, he seeks himself eternally. This seeking is creation, the tail-eater.

Every form of life grows its head from its tail as a transitory revelation of itself, which creates itself from itself. From the primordial spiral of elementary existence rises the vegetative root principle as a primary collective head. From it grows the earthbound, vegetative realm, a spiral tail, a single uninterrupted stream of growth flowing from the root to the crown.

The animal realm, with its individual orientation, is projected laterally by the mobile entity. This lateral projection marks the initial opening of an abstract quality of nature's intelligence, which is self-orientation based on polarity. Reptiles are nothing but a tail that also functions as a head. Its two ends, the root and the crown, are now two poles, positive and negative. The foundation for the crucial conflict between inertial movement and animate intelligence is thus established.

Although based on collective entities, that is, species, the primitive animal head is the bearer of individual consciousness. It acts as the reactive mediator between the abstract, primary vegetative head of creation and its escaping, spiral tail. The animal tail is the natural symbol of this outward growing, estranged root of evolution. It asserts the animal realm, yet like the rudder at the stern of a moving ship, it also manifests a concealed captain.

Instinctive intelligence rules mobility through orientation and evolves as a polarized principle of nature's procreation and sustenance. Male and female, absorbing and assimilating, preaware intelligence sculpts its more and more elaborate tree of command systems. Like a fruit ripening in nature, it finally reaches its Adamic condition of detachment from this original tree. The perfect fruit of nature, which is Adam, is this estranged apple rolling away from its tree, gifted with its own reasoning head, and aware of its conceptual separation from nature. The blind, cyclical force of the primordial tail has rolled away from its head. A spiral of subtle energy, coiled at the root of man's spine, now acts as the reactive psychic rudder. From it an inner flame shoots constantly breaking up into contradictory fiery tongues, reflecting the inverted tail of nature in man. At the stern of man's mental evolution, this tail both asserts and denies his emancipation from nature. Male and female, man absorbs and assimilates nature itself, traveling like a boat through himself, in search of the sleeping ancestor.

Unperturbable, my soul travels silently amid them [the circular lords], entering the Mysterious Shrine, coming forth from the Mysterious Shrine. In the Shrine, it takes what is mine away from those gods of the net of the Lord Tum, for my becoming is prior to him. [*Rev.* 36]

CHAPTER 5

The Dragon's Shrine

I am the one who stills the sky by causing
the earth to tremble. [*Rev.* 5]

The Enshrined Paradox

Expanding and shrinking systems scattered through the
sky, spasms of pain and pleasure which rule earthly
existence—these eerie pulses of life and death remind man
of his own torn heart. He seeks understanding of life like a
diver walking cumbersomely on the bottom of the sea; huge
fish-shaped hopes glide away from his grasp. Looking at
the sky, as into himself, this solitary man, breaking through
the natural hierarchy, sees only empty space, the un-
responding, rotary universe into which his gaze, like an
arrow pursuing its own upward urge, sinks endlessly.

Whereas in nature all creatures obey the harmonic structure which is the mover of universe, in man this inertial,
"tropic obedience" at the root of reason becomes a questioner acting destructively. The evolution of this questioner
uproots nature. He attacks the earth, blindly digging a
labyrinth of dark channels like the worm. With the ceaseless constancy of a primordial pulse, this questioner breaks
up the mental ground of existence, gaining thereby a taste
for self-destruction. Yet, while one part of man's intelligence thus sinks into the ground like a burrowing
worm, another, of which he remains unaware, waits above
it like a blackbird, watching and waiting.

The history of man may be viewed in many different
ways, each of which may be supported by some evidence.
But much of the vital evidence is empirically unobservable.
Like the physical relics of the earth's history crushed into
stone and indistinguishable from mineral, the stages of
man's mental evolution live mutely at the physical core of
his existence. This mute testimony of natural transformations lying at the root of man's intelligence asserts itself as
an unquestionable law. Sealed within its foundation lie the

untraceable affinities between individual and universal life. Founded in nature, man's conceptual intelligence emerges bearing the seal of these affinities. Man can only understand himself if he understands his place in the complex of natural life. Yet his aware reason, as the defining force of this understanding, asserts itself in a separation from nature, although it is one of her parts.

At the root of man's individual intelligence—the natural capacity of man to understand—there is a sealed conflict between the inertia of inanimate nature and animate intelligence: a structurally conceived and physically concealed schism. Through this, man, as a part of nature, rises as an aware separation from her. Although man is able intuitively to feel his natural roots in nature, he cannot naturally preconceive his own intellective evolution from these roots because of this condition of a mental schism which stands, paradoxically, at the origin of his existence and as the conceptual root of this evolution. Thus man is a condition through which nature exalts the coherence of its life and its instinctive behavior by the emergence of conceptual intelligence, which, conceptually, defeats nature through its own force of definition.

> It is I, at the heart of cycles, who am the lord of the lord of the green fields in the beyond. [*Rev.* 15]

The Two Crowns

The structural division of man's brain into the two complementary lobes embodies the root principle of all creation: a qualitative proportion of two unequal dimensions of intelligence from which a third arises as their synthesis. Each cerebral hemisphere is the source of a stream of intelligence, moving as a will through its own domain in man, penetrating his flesh, and seeking its own face. As the line which separates the two sides of man's face joins them into one, so the separation of these two streams of intelligence seek their union in one mental face. One could consider the creation of this mental face as a battlefield holding man's aware "I" *hostage* to its own inner contradiction. As man thinks, so he lives, and as he lives, so he inscribes life into his mind, which is the receiver of the deeds of the doer, who is its own self. The liberation of the hostage is the act of integrating man's two selves. This integration may be seen as a secondary being, rising from man's natural division as from a cross.

> It is I who create the monster of destruction. The scorching blast of her jaws is not turned against me. It is I who ferry the monster, creating her scepter in the midst of her destroyers. [*Rev.* 27]

The Living Cross

Each of the two hemispheres or crowns of man's brain acts as a binary function: the left crown of reason and of synthetic intellect, and the right crown of emotional drives and intuition. Reason, dominating as a fiery red crown of awareness the left hemisphere, and intuition, as a hidden white light of preawareness dominating the right hemisphere, are like the fire of noon and the moonshine of night. The "red crown" of reason acts as an inner opponent to its own sublimation: the "weaver's crown" of the synthetic intellect. Emotional drives react to reason and accordingly reject intuition, their true source. Each continuously projects itself into the other, creating a moving network based upon their fourfold interaction. The left hemisphere commands the movement of the right, active side of man, while the right commands his left, passive side. Since they are interdependent, however, each side receives the reaction of its activity from the opposite side. Each time a brain center is activated, all its reflected activities move too, giving rise to a spectrum of organic correspondences with chains of individual repercussions. Man's mind is free, but its freedom is like a cry lost amid the hills, an estranged, self-amplifying sound, traveling and echoing. It is a new abstract "I," the seer of nature, but also the potential mover of the avalanche.

The two hemispheres of man's intelligence, moving like two blades of a pair of scissors, are connected to the glandular complex which translates their movement through its hormonal chemistry into a contrapuntal fugue of physical movements, moods, emotions, laughter, words, screams, and thoughts.

Two streams of hormonal intelligence constantly shape and sustain man's physical and mental life. Their source is in the contractive pituitary gland, which acts like a potent fire in the center of man's head, and the expansive pineal gland, which, at the back of his head, is like the night herself.

The rational isolation of reason from the warp and woof of its being is the creator of the inverted reflection which is man's conceptual philosophical stand. Trying to be objective, he becomes an object floating aimlessly. Walking on the moon, he finds only black dust, while the moon, which acts as the star-mirror to the earth, escapes his understanding. Studying the close-ups of human bowels and planets, he sees only a magnified minimization of life, while life's structural thought escapes him. He remains the prisoner of his own imagination. Yet, like Jonah, man simultaneously prepares the process of his own regurgitation, the defeat of his objective subjectivism with its mathematical labyrinth.

The evolution of man's rational thought is the observable effect of the unobservable evolution of meaning within his intelligence. Like a mental eye and mental ear, the rational and the intuitive intelligence are woven together on the soul's loom of coherence. Reason acts as a mental "glue"— the structurally deviated soul's cohesion becoming the contractive defining force of the intellect. Intuition acts as the soul's ear of understanding of the mute language of the life-giving thought. This understanding slowly moves man and dissolves the contractive resistance of reason, liberating the eye. The fiery crown of reason becomes the weaver's crown of synthetic intellect.

> I [the hidden weaver] bring together the two crowns within the dweller in his vault. [*Rev.* 23]

Reason and Intuition

As far as we can observe our own mind, we always meet a structure and never an isolated function. Intellective chain reactions seem to constitute a complex that moves throughout the whole body. This moving complex is based upon the cross of intuition and reason.

Intuition and reason are complementary functions, one belonging to space, the other to time. Intuition holds the key to the abstract vision of the simultaneity of all streams of natural intelligence, while reason holds the key to the natural vision of the world felt as exterior to it. Although this latter vision could be called subjective, the former should be thought of not as objective, but as universal. It is only through the universal assimilative "night" of inner cognition that man's reason (the mental force of definition) can function. At the same time, it is only through the subjective capability of definition that the abstract vision can be individually animated.

We can see intuition as an alchemical vessel—the night of

man's transformations—and reason as the alchemical fire of its fermentation. Within the night, fire awakens as a stranger. Within the fire, night calls its dweller to see himself as a torch, as the light-bringer. Thus night acts as a *call* in man and fire as an *announcement*.

Intuition is the irrational call in man, the baying of the dog in the moonlight. But while intuition moves man from within, causing him to seek his soul, and so prepares the way for his transformations, rationality, like the sumptuous, inscrutable cat, eternally seeks its autonomy. Thus just as the dog, although it does not feed on the cat, pursues it perpetually in an irrational search for supremacy, so the force of intuition pursues reason, which flees its authority.

The aware reason is the effect of the structural physiological constitution of man's head. Intuition is its assimilative, animate origin. Reason acts by the laws of physical, digestive movement, which manifest the mental a priori.

Intuition acts as a chemistry of intellective transformations. Reason pulverizes, crushes, dissects, and joins together. Intuition dissolves, corrodes, absorbs, and fuses. In their struggle, intuition and reason split apart, and the variations of their confused aspects are as infinite as numbers themselves. Fighting like eternal lovers and warriors, they build the temple of mind, each stage of whose building is a specific stage, a season in the maturation of their complementation in man's synthetic intellect.

Intuition and reason have both positive and negative aspects. Being two, they have thus four aspects, and their fourfoldness is the field of their culture. Naturally, intuition is the living plower, reason the plow of this field. At first, together they level the ground for the foundation of the temple. But in the evolution of man's awareness, they exchange roles. Reason, becoming the plower, acts unnaturally, as the breaker of his plow: the field is wasted.

> Through his Word he creates his exist-
> ence, yet he does not complete his
> evolution. . . . [Rev. 28]

The Conditioning of Reason

Human reason is a tropic complex, changing its character according to its conditioning, while always remaining the force of definition. In its natural state, as observable in tribal and rural man, reason is conditioned to function within a framework of social codes, in harmony with the environment and its stimuli. Reason tends naturally to lead man to wisdom but only does so if conditioned to move in harmony with its intuitive complement. The conditioning of reason in modern man, however, results not from intuition but from the collective mental orientation of society, manifesting as an inconceivable whole and moving reactively according to the spirit of the time.

> . . . for it is I who re-create the wholeness
> of his body and his soul. [Rev. 28]

The Sacred Island of Transformations

From birth onward, animals grow simultaneously into the use of their bodies and their instinctive intelligence. Man, from birth, grows in two ways. His body grows naturally while his intelligence develops through education. As his intellectual capacity evolves, the child is taught to cut the world into pieces to separate this from that by an individual *name*. Most of the organic perceptions which in animals are directly translated into movements of flight or approach, are filtered by reason in man. It either conducts them into specified areas or rejects them into the sympathetic nervous system, where they are felt as emotions. Thus instinctive motion, caught in the net of reason, is a chained ocean in man and the enemy of its jailer. At the same time, however, emotion, struggling in its net, forces itself into the process of intellectual articulation. In this way, the laws governing the depths of being, which in nature are directly *converted* into cries and muscular movements, are in man transformed into thoughts. Nevertheless, although it is inseparable both from awareness and the drive toward individual affirmation (desire) which orients it, the human intellect, dependent on reason, is naturally separate from the deeper layers of its own consciousness.

> He placed me at the heart of his creation
> to exalt the gods within their shrines.
> [*Rev.* 19]

The Fields of Transformation

As moving streams form patterns of currents within the ocean, so within consciousness, streams of awareness form fields of transformation. Although we cannot clearly separate verbally defined dimensions of awareness, such as psyche or emotion, we can feel their fields of activity in ourselves. Reason, by defining such feelings, erects boundaries within our moving consciousness.

Intellect (the natural balance of reason and intuition), as the thinker within the "I," manifests itself both through reason, as the defining separator, and through intuition, as the conceiver of concepts. In its evolution, intellect disturbs the balance between reason and intuition by creating an ever-greater number of separate concepts, and from these fragments builds a conceptual stand from which evolves its awareness as the negator of the whole. In the midst of its ocean, intellect thus surges as an island. To this island all dimensions of consciousness bring their subtle streams of intelligence to be assimilated into their synthesis: understanding.

The subtle streams of nature's intelligence which belong to consciousness flow from the primary, selective root function of life (absorption and assimilation). Through this selective function life builds its endlessly changing proportional structures of affinity and repulsion forming the net of specific biochemical systems that make up realms and species.

Streams of preaware intelligence have thus solidified into rocks and trees; they became the flesh, claws, and teeth of numberless species through which the elements of the potential synthesis, the human being, gradually form. Within this dark human sanctuary, stars, realms, and species crushed into a memory of their creation surround the two cavities which hold one aware gaze like a spectrum of invisible light.

> For I am the lord of the hidden becoming. I am the limitless. [*Rev.* 37]

The Diver and the Depths

The memory of the one process of self-creation which is inscribed in the abstract "ashes" of all nature's species resting in man's organic codes is moved reactively from within the depths of his consciousness by the hidden "I" of nature, the sleeping king. This moving memory is the soul of a buried "earth-god," an individual, organic "I" hidden from man, yet rising with intellect in him as from his grave. By drawing together his fragmented *members* (the natural functions) into an individual soul—or individualized memory of wholeness—man resurrects as one new born into the eternity of his self-creation. *Man's psychophysical structure* acts like an individual, natural "I," through which the inconceivable "I" of all creation perceives its own creation. Simultaneous and interdependent metabolic cycles of cosmic and natural life merge as vital intellective currents of a thinking structure. They are drawn into a whole by the self-creative, divine awareness of this natural "I" in its continuous transformation.

Like sunlight in the ocean, natural awareness is a thin layer of radiance above the dark abyss of consciousness. The separation of man's awareness from the totality of his consciousness creates fear in him of his unknown depth. Thus he defines the depth as inferior and creates the concept of a *sub*conscious. As a fisherman might try to catch a deep-water fish by slicing away layers of the ocean, man is tempted to try to solve the riddle of his identity by determining the strata of his consciousness as separate concepts.

Far away from the "subconscious" relic of wild beasts, our consciousness shelters its sleeping *knower*, the inner "I," a king unknown to his own kingdom. Streaming from the depths, this ocean penetrates every cell of its own preaware existence, which it rules. Yet something escapes this sleeping monarch of existence: his own offspring, born as his second self-awareness, ignorant of its origin.

Consciousness, a spherical abyss of concentric and eccentric rings turning within separate orbits, is ultimately at the mercy of man, its prodigal son.

The breakdown of the pristine hierarchy of nature and the emergence of the mental "I" of awareness in separation from the natural oneness of intelligence and existence were interpreted in religious language as original sin. Philosophically, this sacrificial *sin* and *fall* can be seen to be the origin of the evolution of man, in whom awareness is destined to be projected as a diver into the abyss of its own origin. By means of this immersion, as if by a fiery baptism, man is absorbed into pain and slowly assimilated into conceptual existence. Meaning, inscribed as the knower and the known in one, closes its circling streams of creation around the intellect, as the eye is closed around its dark pupil.

Glorifying Ra-Atum, I exalt Nu.
[*Rev.* 16]

Awareness and Consciousness

In current usage, "consciousness" and "awareness" are often confused. As I use the word, consciousness is observable both in animals and in man, whereas awareness is observable in man alone. For man can be conscious but unaware of who he is, but the reverse is not possible. In man consciousness acts as a physiological, instinctive, and emotional intelligence reflecting the intuitive force of nature in the psyche. Awareness, on the other hand, is the mystical space of cognition in man, the crown, as it were, of consciousness.

Consciousness moves man's aware, natural reason as the nexus of optical nerves moves his eye to project its gaze outward. Detached from the womb of nature, this aware gaze of the reckoner of nature is projected like a harpoon into the exterior world, only to return like a boomerang, analyzing its own depth, and paralyzing and segmenting the streams of consciousness in an effort to grasp its own self.

Animals have an instinctive consciousness and, in some species, even a primitive form of psyche and reason which have evolved as a command center, allowing a certain degree of individuality, but only within the sphere of the innate behavior of the species. In man, however, intellect rises as a new natural phenomenon. The thinker is able to uproot the instinctive forces which underlie his existence.

Consciousness cannot be divided without injuring its

integrity—yet the process of separation and division is inherent in man. One could say that intellect, as the splitter of consciousness, is the preconceived fruit of the split inscribed in man's original seed. Intellect is the post factum sinner of *original sin*. As such, it develops ever further its own force of separation and reason and thus creates psyche, the natural sufferer. Through its estranged mental eye, reason or intellect tears apart the wholeness of its being, kindling the flame of an emotional reaction which rises from the wound in its own flesh. This relationship between the tearer and the reactive pain marks the rise of the aware second self in man, the mental "I" which cannot identify with anything.

This mental "I," like a sword cutting into its own being, is slowly caught itself in the spasms of pain which it has created. The tearer and the sufferer exchange roles. Intellect becomes obsessed by the pain of its own creation. It can now identify with something, even if it is only pain. By this pain, man's awareness is charged with emotional energy which, in the search for the source of the pain, invokes, like an unadmitted prayer, his wholeness or soul.

> When it sees the red crown, the weaver's crown is exalted. [*Rev.* 30]

The Mystical Reckoner

Beyond reason and intuition, human intellect manifests an individuality whose origin is not traceable to the parental genes alone. *Intellect is the hidden revealer of the wholeness or soul which englobes the spaceless territory of human awareness.* As such, it defines and qualifies the conceptive combination (the Word) of the parental genes. It is the animate, concept "I" of meaning prior to its physical conception.

Aware intellect springs into life as the effect of the preaware premeditation of an intelligence which is not aware, but which reveals itself as the manifestation of the abstract seed of life, that is, life-giving thought. For only thought can create the intelligence which can grasp thought. In conceiving both its natural limitation and its conceptual yet inconceivable origin, intellect opens to life-giving thought. As the mediating "I" of conceptual understanding, intellect manifests the Word rising from the cry. The evolution of intellect is the gradual awakening of the thinker, the radiant salt of evolution, within creation. Radiance rises as spirit. It is the aware uniter of all the constitutional parts of its premeditated eye. In this process of evolution as the aware manifestation of the principle of assimilation, intellect faces its preaware ancestor who is hidden, not in the heavens above, but in blind flesh, denied by reason, his own force of definition. Rising within the psyche of man, intellect manifests the force of aware choice. Being able to identify with reason or reject it, intellect can also accept or reject intuition. Like the mythical Saturn, this mystical reckoner within the centralized system dominated by rationality often acts as the lord of death, yet it is also the force of resurrection. For although indirectly manifesting absorption, the dark hole of psychic hunger in man, rationality, in its separation from intuition, creates the primal mental quality of assimilation which is discernment. One may see the relationship between intellect and its reason depicted in the imagery of Saint George and the dragon. For rationality in man, like the dragon, raises its many heads of inner fragmentation, which intellect must subdue.

I reveal to you, O generations of myself,
that I rule over my creation in the abyss.
For I have seen the abyss becoming I. He
knew not the place in which I became, nor
did he see me becoming his own face.
[*Rev.* 10]

CHAPTER 6

The Stand
in the Abyss

It is I who establish the lords of eternity
for him, I who perpetuate the Mysterious
Shrine in his body. [*Rev.* 33]

The Appointed Time

Through the development of discursive reason within intellect, man's face alters its expression. The urban "intellectual" is recognizable as a new race in humanity. Through reason, psychic hunger rises like a shadow in man and, orienting his emotional craving and mental curiosity, reshapes his face. The trace of expression on a face is the synthesis of the quality of a man's life. Reflecting the balance between his reason and the intuitive cognition of his organic metabolism, man's face is like a planar disk, a cross section revealing the invisible globe of intelligence which contains him.

In man the claw of desire indirectly reflects the hidden, abstract quality of the life-giving intelligence in him. In every human existence, desire acts as the irrational necessity of an evolutive fermentation, the *divine crook*. This crook of the inconceivable "I," the hidden shepherd in man, gathers its flock by first creating its scattered "sheep" and then bringing them together at the appointed time.

My becoming is the crop of the field
which is a desert. [*Rev.* 15]

The Conceiver of Death

A stilled memory of an inconceivable whole lives as a spirit in every speck of existence. In nature, this memory sleeps as the preaware conceiver of its mental conception. In human intellect it awakens as the individual shaper of an abstract intelligence, the eye of premeditation, which grows as a crop within its field.

Being a natural balance between reason and intuition, and thus the field of transformations of the spiritual seed which it naturally manifests, intellect reacts to the complex of reactivities sealed in man by individual heredity and environment. In its evolution, intellect thus conceives death as the mirror of human natural limitation. For although it is the most potent form of intelligence in nature, intellect initially acts as the steering wheel in the hands of a shadow captain—natural reason, which is moved haphazardly by the wind and waves rather than by aware choice. Its assessment of life and creation depends on the conditioning of reason, which in its turn is moved by psychic hunger within the framework of his social structuring and his individual predisposition to hereditary and astrological influences.

This situation of divine intelligence within its progeny, man, creates the *paradoxical imperative of spiritual evolution*. Man's natural reason, the shadow captain, is the key to the shrine of its own animation, but the user of this key, the synthetic intellect, is enclosed in the shrine as a hostage. The shrine is the psyche, a dragon and a womb enclosing the field of transformations that contain the spiritual seed. The opening of this shrine within man is a tortuous, confusing road. In evolving, awareness somersaults, shaking up its original concepts so that new links are constantly created among the parts of the human mind, weaving a new net within it: a net within a net.

In this process man's awareness alters, creating in him a wanderer seeking his home. A fugitive and a rebel upon this long road, he can either destroy himself or stumble upon a new frequency of intellection. This frequency asserts itself as the activation of a channel in awareness that opens intellection to the universal source of his own life. Subtle live frequency, like stellar emanations beaming from a giant eye, pours into man's awareness. Within awareness the channel is the hollow pupil of a different eye. By opening, it draws the void into itself. For it is the "I" which understands its own creation.

The Spirit of Premeditation, untouched by the transformations occurring in its own self, liberates itself from the inert laws of its own becoming. The understanding of the universal principle of creation awakens as the "son" into individual life. Thus the "son" conceives his "father" as the "I" through which the Spirit of Premeditation receives its own radiance. For in man the hidden "I" acts like a lens and a magnet, focusing cosmic and natural languages which converge to emanate the human codes. Seeing its awareness as the hidden *magnet* of its inconceivable self, intellect generates its eye of radiance, the conceiver of life within the conceiver of death. Until that moment, intellect was itself the conceiver of death. In its natural individual awareness, it knew itself to be doomed to die and thus *conceived* mental death.

Although the son of his physical mother and father, each human being as the carrier of intellect is also the effect of a long evolutionary process. He is a meaningless speck of mortal flesh in a faceless universe, yet he is also the "son of God." But even as the "son of God" he is still a speck of flesh like all organic nature, whereas, as the "son of man," as the individual "eye" of the Spirit of Premeditation awakened within intellect, he is the reacher of divinity. For in man, as a time-born species, preaware thought finds its awareness in the living blood of its spirit transmitted through the loom of life as a premeditation. In the universe and in nature this spirit acts as the inert force of premeditation, but in man it divides into preawareness and awareness. Within awareness, out of the blood, steps a stranger, the heir to the divine throne in man's head.

> I rule over my creation in the abyss.
> [*Rev.* 10]

The Negative Absolute

If we plunge into our own mind, searching for our source in the darkness of our being, we reach the limits of our grasp. There the limitless begins. It comes toward us as an endless void, running through our fingers like the water of an all-encompassing ocean. This void is the reflection of our own limitation, the frontier of our intellection.

Relentlessly seeking a rational definition of his origin, man provokes a reactive erasure of definition. It rises in him as the dark whirling abyss rises under his eyelids after he has stared too long at the sun.

This dark frontier is not an ultimate verdict, however, but the transitory name for the inconceivable "I" creating its own negative absolute through man's reason. This negative absolute, as the projection of an incomplete intelligence, acts as a weight on the one side of man's mental balance, provoking as counterweight the rise of emotional unrest. This causes intellect to question its purely rational stand. Man's cognition is a knife with two edges: one is the *no* which defines, the other is the *know* which understands. Every form of knowledge asserts itself as a negative act, provoking its opposite or hidden side. Thus man's rational atheism may be seen as the negative act by which empirical reason builds a foundation for synthetic intellect in its self-created void. Rational intellect sees infinity as a threat to its absolute power of definition and thus interprets it as "nothing" or "void." Yet, in doing so, it rebounds upon itself to face the concept of a true *nothing* which, at the end of its logical line, appears as the negative absolute, the beginning of everything.

For I have seen the abyss becoming I. He knew not the place in which I became. [*Rev.* 10]

The Estranged Shadow

Reaching the status of aware intellect, the human "I," like the immobilized crest of a wave, stares into the ocean of its creation. Although inseparable from its body, it is only conceivable in conceptual separation from it. Although staring like an abstracted eye into its own existence, aware intellect moves man as the wind moves the ocean. Although insubstantial as the wind traversing space and time, it consumes man as fire consumes air.

Unlike hunger, pain, and the inarticulate cries which burst into existence with mouth, bowels, and brain, intellect appears cautiously, like a stranger entering a house. Although coming from nowhere, it makes itself known as the owner of its flesh and disappears at the death of this flesh as mysteriously as it came. Indefinable, it is describable only through its manifestation. As the definer who is one with the definition, it separates itself from itself through description. In this separation, intellect develops its own force of definition, which may be used, like energy, to good or bad ends. This rational "force" grows, indirectly, for the sake of the verbal articulation of man's intuitive cognition.

The rationalized intellect acts as a prodigal arm of the sleeping king. By it, a face of the inconceivable "I" is reactively sculpted in man's mind. Thus the inconceivable "I" emerges from creation as the individual head of the sleeping king, who gathers his mystical body together through the creation of this head and resurrects in the wholeness of his inconceivable self. An individual face is thus created for the inconceivable "I."

I bring together the two crowns within
the dweller in his vault. Thus to the dweller in his vault I bring his own crown. I
draw my kingship from this substantiation. [*Rev.* 23]

Invocation

This premeditated condition of awareness within life, and
not life itself, is the seed bearing womb of life-giving intelligence. *As all organic eggs are not fertilized, so this condition,
although eternally regenerated, is not automatically fertilized in
man, but remains in him as the potential thinker and uniter of the
constitutional parts of his intelligence.*

Man's cerebral structure as the final natural product is the
potential *root* of his transcendence. His awareness rests
upon this physiological structure, which, in its constant
activity, produces a chain of transitory intellective states. It
also acts, beyond its obvious psychic effects, as an invisible
"kaleidoscope," forming reactively the subtle intellective
patterns and frequencies through which human intelligence can always touch on a dimension that is unknown yet akin to it.

In the evolution of human intelligence, when the right
pattern of intellective frequency occurs, the synthetic intellect is activated reactively. The inertial movement of
reason is instantly stilled and drawn into the orbit of its
transformations like a sperm which has reached its ovum.
Through these transformations intellect becomes the self-
conceived dweller in its cerebral vault, the receiver and
definer of the life-giving revelations.

Akin to human breath, life-giving thought, naturally unknown to man, reveals itself as the monarch of his body and
the voice of his soul. Yet this monarch reveals himself only
in response to a mediating mental receptivity, which is the

equivalent of invocation. This involuntary evocation is man's desire to surrender to the desire of wholeness, or soul. Beyond study, discipline, will, or necessity, desire alone can initiate the premeditated germination of the spirit within the closed circle of a natural condition which hides its transcendent root.

At the basis of every observable natural structure, the seed acts as the principle of conversion, and thus also as the principle of the concealing of its unobservable mover, the meaning, within the growing structure.

The creation of life and the evolution of its intelligence, like the root and the stem, conceal the seed of life-giving thought, converting it into the observable living network that manifests the structural principle of the seed's hidden intelligence. This simultaneity of observable and concealed creative movements generates in observable life the seeker of the concealed seed of its awareness.

Awareness rises as the condition of this seeking. Its natural "I" evolves from its preaware premeditation, the human organic seed.

In its spiritual fertilization, awareness steps into a new, destructive phase of its evolution; but in witnessing the painful separation of its intellect from its natural self, awareness generates its new conceptual "I." This "I," as a witness, is also a new eye which brings the estranged eye to its premeditated owner.

> It is I who create the monster of destruc-
> tion. The scorching blast of her jaws is
> not turned against me. [*Rev. 27*]

The Conceptual Inversion

In breaking the established hierarchy of traditional intellective structure, the rise of individual reason may be
seen, like Jonah, as both the victim of the void—the
whale—and as the conceptual intellect's gestation in it. In
establishing palpable experience, reason is swallowed up
by the depths of its origin, yet it acts at the same time like a
plumb line of intellect to measure that depth. Rationality
takes its conceptual stand in the abyss from which, in its
further ramification, it will reach back as a redeemed shadow. Thus it brings about a second reversal of its vision,
which acts as a harmonic corrective to the original reversal
by which man conceived of himself as separate from nature.

In order to invert the established interrelationship of
space and energy, intellect in its evolution must trespass
into an irrational dimension that is beyond earthbound,
observable physical laws. By trespassing into this no-
man's-land, rational intellect goes beyond its own ground,
which is rationality itself. Excitement grows as intellect
breaks through the fixed autonomy of classical laws. By
perceiving mathematically a conceptual relativity of every
form of movement which appears stable against the stability of presumably still space, however, intellect breaks
down the foundation of the established framework of social
hierarchy. A great wave rises in humanity as the awakening
of a new, abstract intelligence. Yet this wondrous wave
breaks and rolls, reaching the earth of its genesis in unequal
tongues of ragged foam. As the wave withdraws into the
sea, its quiescent crest remains like a pool of stagnant water

trapped in the hinterland of the shore. Within this still pool the fermentation takes its toll and a part of humanity is destined for destruction.

> "Your soul rules the flesh of you, O I";
> thus speaks the Self-Creator to me.
> [*Rev.* 34]

The Heraldic Act of Measure

Man is attracted to fiction, to the absurd, to the fearful. This is because as an individual he is insubstantial, fictitious, absurd, and fearful. Yet by approaching his own monstrous self through the maze of mirrors that he is, he is heroic too. His capacity for laughter defeats gravity, lifting him above his condition of being the bearer of nature's pain. In man's awareness the destruction suffered by silent vegetation and unaware animals becomes pain. This pain unites him with the weight of all inert creation, causing the fear of transformations in him and generating destruction. In his constant flight from the inescapable, man breeds violence, rancor, and disgust. In his laughter he embodies all shades of his fear in an unnatural courage.

It could be said that laughter is the true animator of man's individuality, a force equal to procreation. In situations of doom and tragedy, when the absurd is felt as a blind destroyer wiping out intellect and inflaming emotion, man has been known to laugh. This absurd reaction defeats the absurd. It is an irrational act, a gesture of madness. It shakes man's body, producing a triumphant howl like the call of a wild jackal. Yet, in its wildness, it proclaims the triumph of measure over disorder. Laughter, in its ultimate meaning, is the expression of the force of balance that extreme disruption provokes.

Balance rules all existence by measure and by active and reactive force. In man, hidden within the immeasurable depth of his seed, balance holds the genetic codes together and regulates their interrelationship. Thus, this balancing force, beyond man's physical seed, is the creator of the genetic split of consciousness. This split is a proportion, and all living proportion is a self-perpetuating balance. Thus one can see the seat of man's awareness in the split of his consciousness and in the reactive measure of the force of balance which lifts him from nature to counterpoise the inertia of her expansion. Within man, balance has its throne. Through his intellect, it builds its restrictive force, which acts, within its endless cycles of light and darkness, either like a destroyer or like a builder.

Man's awareness is a phenomenon that has no inborn mental code or memory since it is new to nature. Separated from its emotional being, the aware intellect is the denier of its inconceivable "I." Yet, as a part of the force of separation, intellect reveals itself to be an exponent of the measure which rules creation. This may be illustrated by the fact that the most irrational act of balance, laughter, rises in connection with awareness. For it is by the intellectual capacity of observation and comparison that we create laughter.

What is absurd for human beings is not absurd for nature. Nature does not recognize the absurd since she does not generate it. In man, therefore, the intuitive intelligence does not recognize the absurd. Yet, when a man laughs, his instinctive being is reacting to the absurd in the same way as it would to a natural event. A process is thus generated which represents a reversal of the law by which intellect acts as the measurer and interpreter of instinctive forces. By this reversal a concept is lifted out from its cerebral ground. It does not, like other concepts, pass through cortical digestion to emerge as reason or feeling. Instead, it passes directly into the organic realm, asserting itself there as an instinctive reaction, similar to the cry of hunger or fright.

The absurd, as a concept, is the conceptual intellect's reaction to the disorder generated by rationalized intellect. By the act of singling out what is contrary to measure, the intellect recognizes its role as measurer. This recognition is at the base both of mental pain and laughter. People laugh when they are content or victorious to affirm a state of good order. Mostly, however, laughter denounces disorder. It appears to be the protective reaction of an individual against the faceless force of contradiction which denies the established order. Man thus arrives to laugh at himself. By laughing at himself, he denounces a threat linked with absurdity. The more intellect evolves in an individual, the more the laughter of that individual denounces something negative, sinister, or inappropriate which threatens life itself. This threat may not directly concern the individual who laughs, but may concern somebody else, the social order, or even an idea.

Laughter, generated by the experience of the absurd, is the only natural manifestation of abstract intelligence inherent in man. As such, it is a heraldic force and reactive act of measure against disorder. Through laughter, an organic union of aware intellect and its preaware "I" is achieved. Man shakes, screams, barks, and feels relieved, even pacified. In war and disasters, in personal crisis and revolution, one can observe a sudden surge of laughter with its gross vitality balancing the emotional hazards which intellect could alone never control. Or if it could, then it would be a philosophical laughter, reconciling the emergence of the absurd with meaning.

> I am he who brings forth his own
> radiance by offering the force of his self-
> perpetuation to the seed of his divine
> ancestry. [*Rev.* 25]

The Stages of Belonging

Human behavior, based on the awareness of the conceptual separation of individual existence from universal life, reflects the *primary stage of lucidity*.

Like a predator in its den, the aware individual naturally shelters within himself. He moves out like a hunter, following the articulation of his hunger. Yet, unpredictably, incomprehensibly, following his natural hunger, the hunter faces within himself an emotional challenge to his social and moral values, exposing him to something comparable to a slow earthquake. This challenge brings him close to death. He feels a fermentation in himself beyond his capacity to judge its meaning. He feels the limitation of his intellective grasp as a pressure closing down upon him, a menace equal to the physical danger of death. Concepts and ideas seem to open before him like corridors attracting him into indiscriminate exploration. This initiates the *secondary stage of lucidity*, which is the emergence in man's intellect of the concept of the absurd as defining his destiny. Experiencing a standstill in the evolution of his intellect, he shelters in the absurd as the only secure ground. Thus he sustains hopelessness as a new hope. Consumed by hopelessness, he now enters into the *third state of lucidity*, which is the search for meaning.

It is I who create the monster of destruction. [*Rev.* 27]

The Seeker of His Name

Translated into *psychic hunger*, the search for meaning rules man's taste for experience. It grows as an orientating power within the crossing of the threads that are woven in man between earth and sky. The mineral intelligence, which in the crust of its own planet became the seeking flame of the mineral earth and rose into vegetable and animal life, is structurally conditioned to turn upon itself in man, as a self-devouring, insatiable predator.

Man's rational intelligence asserts itself through analysis. It limits: chops up, polarizes, paralyzes, rationalizes, and separates. It annihilates the whole. It assaults the earth and the sky. It is the perfect destroyer. Yet, as it does so, it also builds the power of its hidden "I" to discriminate. Standing between preawareness and awareness, intellect and the thinker, acts as the force of their potential synthesis and as the breaker and harmonic articulator of their natural integrity. Intellect, as the definer through reason, seeks to define the elementary drives that it feels in its organism. It thereby brings them into the maze of its intellective structure, where they wander like lost cries of a hunger which is the seeker of its name.

For when balanced, flames knit together
gods. [*Rev.* 27]

The Conception of Meaning

Endlessly moving, creation follows its repetitive orbits,
sustaining in its rise and fall the ocean of its inconceivable
head. Within this ocean, life stirs like a protozoan foreign to
the water of its animation and yet is inherent, as the hidden
link, in the water's ebb and flow. For organic life represents
steps of proportional reorientation of some of the parts
drawn together within a system of balance to form a new
system of balance growing away from its origin.

The principle of breath, at the root of all existence, manifests in the primordial rhythms caused by gravity which is
inherent in the cosmic system of balance. Ebb and flow
emerge from night and day, causing the vegetative male
and female, which create the animal heart. This heart is
structurally exposed as a system of universal balance in
man's brain. Thus the inanimate system of cosmic balance
behaves like an ever-impregnated womb containing, as the
ocean contains its ebb and flow, the condition for the rise of
the functions or qualities of an unobservable, impregnating
source of animate intelligence.

Containing the visible universe, this abstract womb and
its invisible ferments are only conceivable outside time and
through each other in the germination within the universe
of the inconceivable seed of intelligence, which is prior to
both. This inconceivable seed, beyond chromosomes and
kernels, is the abstract life-giving thought, which, as a
network manifesting the subtle frequencies of its intelligence, connects and harmonizes its life—the stars, constellations, and solar systems which relate to each other like
parts of a huge brain. Scattered planetary systems, unknown to us in the infinity of their life, are billions of "cells"
interacting as one mind beyond our conception of size and
time. Generating specified harmonic frequencies, this life-

giving thought acts as the one seminal intelligence in all the parts of its manifestation.

As the seed of man creates a harmonically moved whole of constitutional and chronologically generated parts which have their own function and yet interact, so the inconceivable seed of intelligence, through which the evolution of man came into existence, generates the harmony of its moving universe in which galactic systems live under their own specific conditions and yet interact. For all specification is a form of translation. Thus specific "unequal" conditions translate meaning into existence, just as words, unequal in their articulation, translate existence into meaning.

All manifestations of life, observable by human intelligence, can only be manifestations of one life-giving intelligence whose specific aspects are reflected in man's aware intellect, arousing the harmonizer of their inert complexity. For only in their own mirror, the aware intellect, can the scattered parts of the one intelligence regain the meaning through which they exist. Owing its existence to a hidden meaning, all existence is but the existence of this meaning, which comes to existence in man, challenging his individual identity. For man's intellect is conditioned through its own existence to seek the meaning of life-giving thought within existence.

One with all parts of its existence, intellect partakes of every function and every movement of its life, both as the definer of life and as its inconceivable "I." By defining life, however, intellect imperceptibly traps itself within a maze of isolated concepts and conflicting ideas. It separates itself from its physical existence to become ghostlike. In separation from its physical existence, intellect causes the awareness in man that his existence has lost its meaning. Yet, before this "loss," gained through its separation from its natural self, intellect did not analyze its existence and thus did not seek its meaning.

> Thus he rises in the sky as the lord of
> gods, who reveals the sky as a radiant
> bloom. Thus, within its opening petals,
> gods gaze at his splendor, the unity of all
> gods. [*Rev.* 19]

The Missing Link

One could say that the meaning of existence comes into
being as the missing link in the intellect of man when he
becomes aware of the absurd split between his mind and
body. The experience of the absurd may thus be taken as
the conception of meaning within man. It is the reversed
image of wholeness and thus its preconceiver. The absurd
is only human, like meaning itself. In humanity, however,
it is not natural like love, fear, and joy. At its appointed
hour it rises in the evolution of man's intelligence as the
force of seed gathers in the autumn. This element of *timing*
suggests a premeditated process of mutation that has ger-
minated during the natural season of harvest. During the
critical period in which seasonal leaves wither and hungry
beasts haunt the foodless forest, the menace of death
appears as the reverse face of a promise of the new spring
held within the earth. And whereas in the earth this seminal promise, like a preying crocodile, awaits in stillness its
appointed hour to burst into action, in intellect this promise
of new life appears, by virtue of the absurd, as a sinister
force, generating both suicidal depression and humor.

Through humor the split between scattered, observable
facts and the inner desire for meaning becomes a mover,
resurrecting the paralyzed life-force and thus hooking
together its disconnected parts. One could compare this
reemergence of life from paralysis to the emergence of a
new species. For it is no less wondrous to see the absurd
translated into laughter in a grieved man than it is to see

hair emerging on the cheeks of a boy, or fur or wings appearing in a new species.

Man understands instantaneously through the same order of reintegration as that through which he assimilates absorbed substances and instantly reintegrates them as elementary affinities into the functional parts of his organism. Similarly the evolution of nature's intelligence summarizes the completion of its qualities in a sudden mutation. Such completion instantaneously draws together its scattered parts from the whirlwind of creation, like a sudden outcry or burst of laughter. Completed in stars, animals, plants, and stones, the wandering, invisible cuckoo-egg of intelligence travels from species to species as an impostor and mediating seal-bearer through whom a chain is forged between earth and sky.

As the synthesis of the long, natural genesis of man's constitutional parts, the aware intellect, although emerging as a separation from man's preaware being, reveals the "I" of an irrational cohesion—or soul—as it attracts its constitutional parts to itself like a living magnet creating coherence within awareness. It is the separating frontier which links preaware nature and awareness as two different qualities of human intelligence to their precreational wholeness. Through intellect, analysis is born and also the reintegration of separate parts which spring together into a new whole.

> I am the true lord of the seal of the house
> of crushing, for I sum up my multiple
> shapes. [*Rev.* 18]

The Seal

Man is both the product and the creator of the stages in the
evolution of his intelligence. His reason as the dominant
exponent of his centripetalism is also the necessary tool by
which he may extract himself from his natural mental attitude. Although it is often said that man is ruled by his
animal instincts, his reason, due to its interpretation of
events, causes these animal instincts to rise in disorderly
fashion and makes him emotionally unbalanced. Such a
man steps out of his natural and social framework and,
becoming solitary and bitter, repels his own society, which
defends itself against intensely inquiring individuals. As a
thinker, man is thus brought to the door of an inner
transformation. While he evolved as a social individual
through success and failure, now he evolves philosophically, through his understanding. When the condition for a
new stage is generated in him he acts as a destroyer and his
world becomes like the Western world today, the stage for
destruction. Curled in a corner of the hollow tree of his
solitude, the Western intellect sinks into a corrosive, gra-
tuitously nihilistic state of mind, such as is unknown to
nature. Yet, like a magnet, it attracts and dominates a
multiracial mass of individuals who leave their natural sur-
roundings to congregate worshipfully around it. This paradoxical situation reveals that man, without regard for good
or evil, seeks such relationships and situations as will pro-
voke his own transformation. The dangerous shadow of
this search for transformation is the establishment of a
self-destructive mentality as the negative echo of the extreme disruption of order. Pornographic eroticism, for in-

stance, stands in direct opposition to laughter, which is an affirmation of the absurd. Whereas laughter negates the impact of the absurd on the psyche by pacifying unrest and joining body and intellect, eroticism does the opposite. It affirms the absurd, widening the gap between existence and meaning. Draining nervous energy into its abyss, it causes sterile tension and promiscuous morbidity. The search in the human being for the right *tension*, even at the cost of his security and happiness, corresponds to the slow contractions by which a larva seeks the utter darkness of a hollow tree to perform its primordial metamorphosis. Choosing the right orientation, it wraps itself up like a mummy in its own secretions, giving itself up to a process unknown to itself—a process which, as a larva, if it could think rationally, it would call death. Man unknowingly follows the same primordial ritual of inhumation, giving himself to the utter darkness of a mystical sacrifice. Through his mental attitudes, man seals around his own heart a hermetic chamber; like a mummy he isolates himself within the emanations of his intellect. Isolating himself for his mystical dissolution in a mental space, he commits the supreme act of a will unknown to him. Sinking into his self-created void, man stretches himself out as a bridge between nature and her abysmal root, which now germinates through intellect as a new force. For while one side of his intellect, like a jackal, pulls him down into a whirlpool of intestinal darkness, another, like a dancing dwarf, springs up in response, perilously somersaulting over the abyss.

Breaking open the ancient hermetic seal, intellect may be seen as the germination of a new seed. As the breaker of the ancient jar of cohesion, intellect today spills the holy water. It flows forth like a burning flood. Yet this flood is an insemination. By it a new name is forged in humanity: the water-carrier.

They see the Self-Creator, called forth by me, as he emerges from the one in whom they have prepared my way. By such *seeing*, I surge from the Mysterious Shrine as he who creates himself. [*Rev.* 31]

CHAPTER 7

The Birth of Meaning

I became the weaver in the flesh of the ancestor who creates himself from himself. [*Rev.* 11]

The Hidden Weaver

Words surge forth as a result of a process through which certain parts of the brain absorb multidimensional information reducing them to mental "ferments." These cause the chain reactions that stand at the root of thought and behavior. Reaching the ambience of their activation in the brewing bowl of man's head through a process of affinity and repulsion, the mental ferments, extracted from nature as abstract intelligence, become the stimuli of the organically inscribed natural memory of universal creation. Within this organic *memory*, movements and thoughts are guided to respond to stimuli. These responses, rising in consciousness, manifest themselves to man, clearly or unclearly, as emotion, physiological activity, cry, or aware word.

Absorbed into certain parts of the brain through the agency of the sense, these ferments are passed on as mental *chyle* to other parts of the brain, where they are assimilated into the texture of the psyche and affect all levels of man's life. For whereas in the animal's brain a constant reactivity alone determines behavior, in man's brain there is also a hidden weaver who creates a cloth of conceptual intelligence. This intelligence absorbs information during the day and digests it during the night. Without his aware participation, man's mind assimilates absorbed information according to the quality of his psychic hunger. From the night of man's consciousness, an indefinable intelligence acts as the receiver and the analyzer of information, breaking it up into elements of a preaware, organic language and storing these in the appropriate centers of the brain, thus fostering the "day" of his verbal definitions.

We could say that this hidden "I" rules man's awakening

by its sleep and rules his sleep by its awakening. Aware reason, as the dominant force of man's intelligence, influences the way in which his mind acts in its sleep. We can also say that in sleep, intuitive intelligence reacts to man's behavior, caused by his reason, and thus influences its state of awakening. The hidden weaver not only acts in this way through preaware and intuitive warnings, or through the dream imagery in sleep, but also fosters man's aware thoughts that are never purely intuitive or purely rational but always express a degree of interaction between his preaware and his aware self.

Unknowingly trusting intelligence (this hidden weaver), man often sleeps on a problem when he wants to make sure of the right judgment. This natural way of balancing reason and intuition is disturbed, however, by the unnatural complexity of problems arising from the development of rational thought over and above intuition. Reason, as the dominant force of man's mind, acts as a reductionist in its interpretations, regardless of emotional consequences. Estranged from its intuitive source, this reactive emotion often engenders a reactive hunger for suffering.

The degree of synthesis between intuition and reason in intellect dictates the quality of the psychic hunger in man. It is this hunger, whether it be positive or negative, and not the opinions of the personality, which as the hidden force of desire creates the will in human reason, which blindly shapes the mystical eye of intellect. Like the harpoon in the hands of the Spirit of Premeditation, psychic hunger transfixes man's heart, causing him to suffer the experience of contradiction, through which the "eye" of synthesis is born.

Every man may be understood as an individual seal, holding captive the preaware seal-bearer, the intellective spirit of the hidden "I," which is beyond physical form or existence. This hidden "I" is the Spirit of Premeditation acting as the conceiver of its premeditated, conceptual existence.

This nonsituated, abstract, but ever-present spirit holds the handle of its own loom and, the master of tension, upholds man's psyche as the mental cloth of its own creation. Within that loom, man's destiny often seems ruled by destruction. Yet regardless of the apparent state of man's mind, the Spirit of Premeditation acts until a certain degree of communication occurs between his intuition and reason as the unchosen imperative of the reactive patterns of his behavior. At this point the psyche gains the desire to question its own hunger. Questioning the unchosen imperative of this existence, man enters into aware contact with the hidden chooser, which is the Spirit of Premeditation. Thus, the unchosen is revealed as chosen.

> I make those who follow light stand erect, as his very legs. I become his risen arms. [*Rev.* 13]

The Wound of Transcendence

The hidden wound dividing our mind into two interacting intelligences is the mystical foundation of our intellect. Pain is an unchosen endless division and yet the revealer of the whole. Human life is an abstract twofold spiral based on a fixed proportion of their relationship, which conditions its structural propagation within the limits of the individual master plan, of air being impressed in it.

The human skull is a vault. It has openings for ears, eyes, nose, and mouth and for blood and spinal marrow. Through these openings, subtle streams of intelligence circulate and cross, creating a labyrinth which one can visualize as a rotating spider's web. In its center—instead of the spider—there is a seesaw upon which a shadow and a ghost are fighting. Each endlessly tries to knock the other down but loses its balance, for although fixed at its center, the seesaw moves unpredictably.

An irresistible call in every thinker draws him to project his awakeness into the maze of its roots. Following this projection, the thinker reduces himself to an intruding object. Like a thorn which has penetrated flesh, he stands neutralized in the midst of the inflamed circle of his own brain. Within this circle, man faces the two opposing selves himself. Thrown from one side to the other, he becomes unable to bear the escalation of the conflict, which has been naturally generated, but cannot be naturally resolved. Thus, he experiences crucifixion. In his empirical evolution, man, perpetuating its cross, embraces the wheel of his torture like a medieval martyr.

> It is I who ferry the monster, creating her scepter in the midst of her destroyers.
> [*Rev.* 27]

The Hole and the Whole

Psyche is naturally conditioned to inquire into itself. Yet this inquiry leads psyche to analyze its acts, creating an unnatural, analytical mentality that amplifies the effects of its self-inquiry, generating an abyss in man. Afraid of this enclosed, all-absorbing inner precipice, man turns to an exterior abyss greater than himself. In front of the infinite universe or sky which surrounds him, he becomes either a rational nihilist or the irrational seeker of a ladder which will link him to an imaginary fixed point, a divine hook beyond empirical perception.

Through rationality, the thinker sinks and is absorbed into the depth of his own being, and he interprets his emotional reaction to this sinking by conceiving of the depth as a *hole*. By trying to limit its intuitive reactions, reason in the seeking thinker gives rise to new, unnatural emotional states, which it then defines through new concepts. These concepts that have been generated in him by the preaware net of affinities and through which the thinker can judge his experience, he terms "objective." *Thus rationality creates an imaginary, exterior criterion as the rational basis for a philosophical form of irrationality, a nihilism rooted in an irrational yet naturally induced mental attitude.* This attitude, through which psychic hunger manifests, then becomes the trigger of his actions. Thus, at the root of his mental and physical appetites and as the dominant force of his awareness, reason activates the two arms of the extreme points of intellective balance: rational objectivism and irrational hope. Between these two he swings like a pendulum, suspended over the vortex of his own creation.

When rationality proclaims the absence of an empirically observable spiritual presence within its psyche, it places, following the unchosen a priori of logic, the concept of objectivity in its place. Thus, for rational man, objectivity, to which he clings, acts as the replacement—if only in its quality of judge or negator—of the missing spiritual hook. This negation of spirit, in the classical sense, is reason's negative enthronement of divine authority, now reduced to the rational dimension. Unable to understand the totality of the language of intuitive cognition, reason naturally negates the possibility of a dimension of intelligence different from its own. However unknowingly, reason thus creates the unnatural abstract shell from which the "artifact" of intelligence, synthesis, can evolve.

In man, rational judgment must act through experience, while experience cannot understand its feeling without judgment, which, however, is a separation from it. Man intuitively feels *space* to be a womb of potential substantiation, yet empirically he defines it as a void. His understanding of life is then imprinted on this psychic void as the reflection of sky and trees are imprinted upside down on a forest pond. In his yearning to fuse with this abstract reflection, man creates a psychic eye as a ghost rising from its self-created void. In other words, man encloses a self-created void within his natural intellect. Within this enclosure, synthesis grows like the luster of a pearl within its opaque shell.

> Through his Word he creates his existence, yet he does not complete his evolution, for it is I who re-create the wholeness of his body and his soul.
> [*Rev.* 28]

The Hearer

The evolution of the thinker through nature and man may be seen as a ladder whose rungs are partly hidden and partly observable. The rungs are the scale of the time-generated natural stages of species. Time in evolution is like the stomach in man. It interacts constantly with both its hidden foundations and with its immeasurable height, its head. *The rising scale of organic intelligence, with all its time-bound processes, does not bring about its final fruit in man, but only the condition for fruition which is beyond man's natural grasp.*

By means of time, the Spirit of Premeditation acts as the regenerator of the self-created flesh of its thought. Thus it sustains the temporal laws which, in turn, sustain within the rise and fall of matter the gestation of the thinker destined to enter into timelessness. This gestated self, rising from its time-born humanity, reveals its own face by conceiving itself as the awareness of meaning, extracted from its premeditation. Thus, through space and time, meaning reduces itself to definition. Through that "sacrificial" act at the root of all seed, pure divine awareness separates from itself as the conceiver of the oneness within this separation. To conceive itself as one, the "I" generates its existence, a system of balance, the universe. This system of balance, reflected in human awareness, gathers together all its functional parts within this reflection into one synthesis, the aware Word of the "I," which thus *sees* its own self as one. The joy of the recognition of self by its estranged self is the engendering cry of divine existence, continually generating meaning as its own self-conception. Thus the self-generation of meaning through physical existence cannot be placed in time, however much it may appear so. Meaning, within the divine self, is a constitutional part of the inconceivable "I," as our natural process of thought is a constitutional, inseparable part of our "I." For this reason, human existence represents the axis of the self-creation of meaning within its inconceivable "I."

Eternal and self-created, meaning, in its pure state, radiates and beams into its Spirit of Premeditation, exhaled by its inconceivable "I." Impregnated with meaning, the Spirit of Premeditation sinks into its premeditation, which emanates from its inconceivable self. Within creation it acts, at the core of all seed, as the seed of seeds.

Preaware and aware meaning are the source and the mouth of creation: the cry and the Word. The Word of the words is the radiant eye of premeditation, one with all its aware, man-generated words, its selves. Uncreated and eternally whole, the radiant eye of premeditation is the divine, spiritual sun of pure awareness, one with the inconceivable "I" and the self-creation of its conceptual selves, as our awareness is one with our "I" and all our thoughts.

The aware Word, embracing its divine awareness, is the guardian of its self-regeneration throughout the cycles of its existence. It is, as such, equally close to its dual force of life and death. For seed, although memory of wholeness, is definition, and so veils its original wholeness, which is undefinable, through a system of balance in which creation and destruction act equally as the proportional parts of its wholeness. Within the limited framework of its definition, *the seed is at once the life-force and the death-force, which conceives life, not limitlessly but as a limitation. It is this contradiction that creates its mirror of despair in the mind of man.*

Despair in man is the animation of the self-limiting force of the genetic memory of life. Despair, in its reactive clash with the stirring of its intelligence, is inertial movement woven into the search for its limitless "I." Inertial movement, as the only observable mover of life, is the shell of an invisible egg containing the potential life-giving thinker. This potential thinker is the "salt" of evolution, the "ear" of the inconceivable "I" in all substance, attracting like a magnet its own "voice" captured within its memory. Following this voice, the "I" forges all organic blueprints, thus shaping its creation from within. Beyond the inertial movement and cellular tropism by which its orders are carried out in every life form, this "ear" is the preaware law-giver, subject in its sleep to its own law. From the base of man's being, this "ear" stirs, creating within its own abyss as the stages of its "hearing," the evolution of man's mental eye. From one point of view, this hearing is the summit of nature's evolution; it represents the fruit of the process of the structural centralization of preaware intelligence: the individually aware, thinking brain. The evolution of awareness from this centralized mentality proceeds, however, as a process of decentralization, breaking up preaware intelligence. Thus awareness emerges as a separation and a clash, whereby conceptual existence, the existence of meaning, is forged.

The human mind can only understand itself if it conceives of itself as a structure in which many forces interact according to a proportional measure which is their oneness. Thus the concept of the "subconscious" as a disorderly, inferior realm yields to that of a highly organized, preaware intelligence, linked to its awareness in the same way as a root is linked to its stem. Awareness flowers, and in its fruition it sinks down again into the foundations of consciousness, thus exalting its preaware roots in the cognition of its seed. This reimmersion is a gradual process brought about by the structural law ruling man's brain and reflecting the harmonic proportion between an unknown "tonic" and its seeking "dominant."

As the dominant force of awareness, reason is the natural interpreter of all sensory information. At a certain stage of natural evolution, reason, like a flower, faces its withering. Its empirical force of definition dissects the wholeness of life, creating the foundations of an unnatural emotional experience. Within this experience, intellect rises as the forbidden fruit which consumes yet also digests and assimilates itself, becoming its hidden seed.

The evolution of the thinking capacity in man and his individual chance to control his destiny by it depends upon the ratio between his awareness and his preaware consciousness. Through this measure his intellect evolves, acting indirectly within its womb of consciousness in its true function as a spiritual seed.

The evolution of life in the universe, like the tree in its seed, represents a ramification of life-giving intelligence, whereas *the evolution of awareness in man represents the passage of this ramification into self-cognition.*

Thus he forges me to create his heart and
sends me forth as his radiance. [*Rev.* 14]

The Mysterious Shrine

In the moving stillness of its spiral of continuous self-
creation, the inconceivable "I" is the essence of life. Awake,
it is the radiant eye of the Spirit of Premeditation. Asleep, it
is the rising spirit within creation.

In the very instant of its awakening within its self-
generated body, it becomes the imperishable eye, the
generator of radiance which is its seed and of light which is
its Word. Its true revelation is a cry of new life bursting forth
within the tear of a generative completion (death). Through
this completion, radiance regenerates meaning in the universe. It is the mender of destroyed order, the healer of the
sick, the potter within the clay. It is the hidden revealer in
the human mind. Through revelation, it reaches its own
self in man and emerges within psychic existence as a
dweller in its insubstantial egg. It evolves as a response of
the sleeping king to the human invocation of meaning. This
human invocation of its conceiver sculpts its own face within the natural face of man: the face of the subtle dweller, the
man-born Word.

The man-born, aware Word acts as the light within the
radiance of stars. Through affinity it generates its own
shadow in those who seek to see it. In them, it fosters its
own "kind." It dwells, unseen, in sacred books and images,
in statues and trees, waiting to enter man through its two
portals, intuition and reason, thus opening them as a single
entrance of light into the human being. This entrance un-
seals the shrine immured in man, the generative space of
the mystical heart of intelligence.

Word is enshrined in every human being, as a nonsub-
stantial sanctuary, the mystical head. Enclosed in the tem-

ple of the flesh, the unborn breath, exhaled by its inconceivable "I" reemerges as its own conclusion. Conclusion is the meaning within the Word, self-generated by human awareness in search of its origin. Conclusion is the peak of every life, and in death it is the opening of the holiest shrine from which breath escapes into a new genesis. When awareness reaches its peak, it encompasses creation and, as a still lightning, merges into radiance, escaping time. With this consumed instant, which is the generative space of meaning, time itself ceases. The fruit of its generation has filled it, as the child fills the womb.

From sleep to its awakening, one intelligence thus perpetuates within its spiral becoming its ever-evolving, ever-changing dweller. Moving like blood around its invisible heart, radiance beams perpetually into its own circling foundations. Thus life-giving thought evolves into awareness and, as the living Word-god, reaches its conclusion, which is the generative end and the seminal beginning. Its inconceivable "I" can only be evoked in us by its reflection and felt as the emotional reality within our heart, which we name God.

Thus the blood of God streams around God, being one with God. It is the origin and substance of the word by and through which God is one with all his farthest corners. When a child trips and falls, it is God who falls; when a man spits venom, deafened to reason, he carries his own fright like the falling child who is the inarticulate God. For time is the lord in the field of divine articulation and pain is its minister. Pain penetrates, shrivels, and moves nature in this field which is man.

Thus, united with the desire of life which becomes love of death, man pulls the strings of time, the great self-exterminator. Pain is the distance between the two hands of God working against each other in the mind of man. In man, pain lifts itself out of the earthquake, its foundation,

becoming the singing voice of God, one with sorrow, one
with the mother who gives birth, one with the cry of the
born, one with the dying father, one with the bride and
bridegroom, one with the beggar, one with the road, and its
inseparable, ever-lasting wanderer.

> For I am the lord of the hidden becom-
> ing. I am the limitless. [*Rev.* 37]

Appendix

THE REVELATION OF THE SOUL OF SHU
A New Translation from the Ancient Egyptian
by Bika Reed

Translator's Note

From the scattered inscriptions of ancient Egypt rises a body of abstract, creative thought which, like the mythical dismembered king Osiris, awaits resurrection in the living mind. Egypt left behind scriptures which by the quality of thought prove not only a long lineage of culture unknown to us and predating archaeological evidence, but also the existence of an unchangeable spiritual essence: the existence of meaning within ourselves. This essence lying at the core of awareness can be stirred into activity like a seed in its field.

The Revelation of the Soul of Shu, as presented in this book, is a new translation from ancient Egyptian into English of an inscription, found in the coffin of Gwa, now in the British Museum. Gwa was a physician of the 12th Dynasty, a learned nobleman, and his coffin, like those of all noble Egyptians, has been entirely covered with writing.

The Revelation of the Soul of Shu cannot be read without an effort of concentration and some preliminary knowledge of the ancient Egyptian way of thinking. For instance, in current speech, we use personal pronouns in order to separate: I am such-and-such, you are someone else, he is different from both me and you, and they are a mass of unknown people. In her sacred texts, Egypt changes the natural use of words, especially of pronouns. We often read phrases such as "I am he" or "he is I." Logically speaking, these phrases yield no sense, and they are often corrected by Egyptologists. But Egypt speaks between the lines. Unsaid meaning, created indirectly, is not a secret. The purpose behind the abnormal use of words is not to hide the truth but to reveal it.

By giving a pronominal existence to forces and cosmic functions, mythical thought artificially creates a natural bridge between the thinker and the abstract principles of creation. We may be allergic to the idea that our physical organs have their corresponding mental selves in our minds, but we can eventually experience to our own amazement the inner reality of the "he" and "she" who act in our name under different circumstances. Different "people" act in ourselves in different relationships, as different gods act in the universe according to different set patterns or laws. Becoming aware of the unchosen imperative of the inner reality of all existence, one can gradually discover the wonder of wholeness and begin to act in it as the harmonizer, the awake eye which is an I of the Self-Creator.

Basically, the vision emerging in man as an awake eye within its field of transformations enters gradually through the door of something close to terror: the unchosen imperative of existence is like a chessboard, a net of inexorable action-reactions. The pawns are blind impulses and the players are undefined. Our intellect conceives the fact that there are two players in every game: nature plays for kingship and power; the awakening priest of intellect plays to win that kingdom for his lord Shu. This inner reality of a field of transformations is depicted in a papyrus in which a lion (the king of nature) and a unicorn (the redeeming awareness) play the ancient Egyptian version of modern chess.

The Revelation of the Soul of Shu is one of the rare texts containing the self-re-creative thought which is able to resurrect in the reader and become the guide of his spiritual evolution. It may seem strange in a civilization which fears death that anyone should hope for life from coffin-wisdom. But each ancient Egyptian coffin-text is a spiritual seed for survival beyond fear of death.

The tombs of sages were shrines to which initiates were brought to receive such seeds of spiritual culture. While temples provided knowledge essential for the education of spiritual masters, tombs held the key to the practical application of this abstract knowledge: every stage of growth needs—in spirit as in nature—a specific kind of sustenance. Tombs alone provide wisdom that has been absorbed and assimilated through a human life. Every tomb is a seed of the awakening of Osiris in man. Every coffin, with its particular combination of spells, is an individual "gene," a seal and seed in one. So we find in the tomb of Methethy, one of the great spiritual masters of Egypt, an address to all who would come to his tomb:

> To every one of my brothers, men who yearn for eternity and come to bring their offerings to my tomb, I shall give mastery over invocation of divine birth within the tomb.

The Revelation
of the Soul of Shu

1. *The Revelation of the Soul of Shu*, about the coming forth of Shu.

2. I am Shu, the creator, coming forth from his own self. I come forth through my utterance as the ruler of the flesh created from its own self.

3. I am the soul of Shu coming forth in the members of the one who creates himself from his own emanations.

4. In the flesh of the one who creates himself, it is *I* who am edified, for my coming forth is his being.

5. I am he who stills the sky by causing the earth to tremble.

6. I guide the one who evolves from the eternal rise and fall. For him, I bind the knots, the divine reintegrators of his own name.

7. I am the dweller within the million beings. I gain awareness from the million beings. I disseminate, to his own generations, the word of the one who creates himself from himself.

8. I am the one great in the mastery of the functions of his vessel. My strength and potency are greater than all powers.

9. Strong and powerful, it is I who am the origin of all gods. For I reinstate the word of the ancestor of all creation as the generative law and begetter of his own *generations*, which will perform my evolution through the ocean of time. They [these generations] will identify my restrictive forces with the great mystical ship, steered by him who liberates his being from his own self. I shall rise to power in them, from within, to give him [the ancestor] the redeemer of his body through my genesis.

10. I shall call out: Silence, Lords of Time, issued forth from the ancestor of genesis. I reveal to you, O generations of myself, that I rule over my creation in the abyss. For I have seen the abyss becoming I. He knew not the place in which I became, nor did he see me becoming his own face.

11. I became the weaver in the flesh of the ancestor who creates himself from himself. He forged me to create his heart. He emanated me to become his radiance. He exhaled me to become his nose. I am *"This"* which breathes creation.

12. I establish the Lord "This" to exalt the Self-Creator and reveal the sky as his inherent power and the unity of all creative laws. Thus, inconceivable to the gods of creation, he edifies his name.

13. I make those who follow light stand erect, as his very legs. I become his risen arms.

14. Thus he forges me to create his heart and sends me forth as his radiance. Unborn, I am older than birth itself.

15. My becoming is the crop of the field which is a desert. It is I who bake the divine bread. It is I, at the heart of cycles, who am the lord of the lord of the green fields in the beyond.

16. Glorifying Ra-Atum, I exalt Nu. It is I who regenerate substance to restore the animator of the holy flesh of Osiris. Gods, hidden in their shrines, fear him.

17. I regenerate the offering to restore the *animator* of the divine flesh. I come forth in the flesh of the Lord "This" to restore his being and reveal the sky as a full bloom— the oneness which sums up all creative laws.

18. I am the true lord of the seal of the house of crushing,* for I sum up my multiple shapes.

19. I am the breath of divine creation. I did not spring from his utterance, nor did he engender me by semen. He exhaled me to create his nostril. He placed me at the heart of his creation to exalt the gods within their shrines. Thus he rises in the sky as the lord of gods, who reveals the sky as a radiant bloom. Thus, within its opening petals, gods gaze at his splendor, the unity of all gods.

20. In the Self-Creator, it is I who am the breath of all creatures. Older than his vegetating fields, in the sanctuary of the Holy Six, I am at the root of mysteries.

---

* The "house of crushing" refers to the constrictive rationality of the intellect.

21. I have forged my soul which gave me birth, for older than its revelation am I, the Knower. My soul shall not burn with my body. My soul shall not be dismembered by the guardians of the wholeness of the flesh of Ra.

22. I forge my soul in creating the concept of my soul within the dwellers of the Lake of Fire. Thus I conceive myself through the gods, whom I carry as my crown.

23. I bring together the two crowns within the dweller in his vault. Thus I bring the dweller in his vault his own crown. I draw my kingship from his substantiation.

24. I do not obey spells. I precede them. It is I who give breath to life which surges from the Word of Tum, for he comes after me. I am the ever-evolving Self-Creator, the sole one who is older than the gods.

25. I am he who extends the heights of heaven. I am he who brings forth his own radiance by offering the force of his perpetuation to the seed of his divine ancestry.

26. I have extinguished the flames. I have subdued the fiery monster. I have made her quiet in the midst of her destroyers: For when balanced, flames reassemble the gods.

27. It is I who create the monster of destruction. The scorching blast of her jaws is not turned against me. It is I who ferry the monster, creating her scepter in the midst of her destroyers. For when balanced, flames knit together gods.

28. O gods, your mind does not evolve through your own utterance, but through me alone. My becoming is the force of the entire creation, which flows forth from the

Word of the great Lord "This." Through his Word he creates his existence, yet he does not complete his evolution, for it is I who re-create the wholeness of his body and his soul.

29. It is I who rule the rulers of the tomb and put fear into the servants of the Mysterious Shrine. They prepare the way for me. Thus I sink into the Shrine and surge from it as he who creates himself.

30. I have drawn onto my head the weaver's crown. The red crown sees it.* On my head, the weaver's crown is the red crown on the head of the Self-Creator, for when it sees the red crown, the weaver's crown is exalted. Their voices unite. The divine mind awakens to their words and becomes one with the Self-Creator, in his own flesh.

31. They see the Self-Creator, called forth by me, as he emerges from the one in whom they have prepared my way. By such *seeing*, I surge from the Mysterious Shrine as he who creates himself.

32. I rule those who rule fatality. I realize the realizer. I sustain the sustainer. I destroy the destroyer, for I abominate destruction.

33. I am one with the Lord of Life. I unify his multitude. I bind together his gods. It is I who establish the lords of eternity for him, I who perpetuate the Mysterious Shrine in his body. By my will, after me he forges the oracle of my soul for me. For prior to its revelation, I am the knower. I am the measure of heaven. I permeate all lands. I create his will in me.

* The weaver's crown" refers to the synthesis of reason and intuition. The "red crown" refers to reason alone.

34. He will not let my soul be consumed, in my dismembered flesh. No guardian of the mysterious shrine will touch my soul. "Your soul rules the flesh of you, O I"; thus speaks the Self-Creator to me.

35. My soul shall not be caught by the hawks. My soul shall not be eaten by the devourer of the dead. My soul does not serve the gods who work the net for catching souls. My soul does not honor the gods of magical spells, those circular lords of eternity.

36. Unperturbable, my soul travels silently amid them [the circular lords], entering the Mysterious Shrine, coming forth from the Mysterious Shrine. In the Shrine, it takes what is mine away from those gods of the net of the Lord Tum, for my becoming is prior to him. His arm (of self-destruction) is my scepter in my enemies in the sky or on the earth. I expel them from their hidden place. I overthrow them in their fortress. I destroy them from within their own base. I break their authority from within their establishment. I transfix their vital force. I dismember their mind. I reduce them to slavery.

37. Thus the Self-Creator ordains for his enemies, dead or alive, in sky or earth, who tread my plantation in my field, refusing to exalt me, and not preparing for me the way to liberation. For I am the lord of the hidden becoming. I am the limitless.